If you want to	See pages for Shell method		
DOS Shell (Start)		7	dosshell
Drive (switch to)	27	28	*drive:*
Edit a text file	125-134	125-134	edit
Environment (view)			set
File (look for)	32-33	34	dir
File (look in)	55	55-56	type
Format a disk	60	61	format
Help (on commands)		22-24	help *or* fasthelp
Help (on DOS Shell operations)	17-18		press F1
Hide file	56	57	attrib
Input data to batch file		143-147	choice
Label disk electronically	60		label
Laptop (conserve battery power)		123-124	power *or* power.exe
Memory (optimize)		107-110	memmaker
Memory (check available)		106	mem *or* msd
Move directory	68-69		
Move file	52-53	53	move
Multiple configuration (create)		135-142	help multi-config
Path (specify)		150	path
Pause screen scroll		86-87	more *or* Ctrl+S
Print file		84-86	print *or* type
Print output		83	*command* >prn
Prompt (change)		28	prompt

The Up & Running Series from SYBEX

Other titles include Up & Running with:

AutoSketch™ 3

Clipper® 5.01

Flight Simulator®

Harvard Graphics 3

Harvard Graphics for Windows

Lotus 1-2-3 Release 3.1

Windows™ *3.1*

Word for Windows 2.0

WordPerfect 5.1 for DOS

WordPerfect 5.1 for Windows

XTreeGold™ 2

Computer users are not all alike.
Neither are SYBEX books.

All computer users learn in their own way. Some need straightforward and methodical explanations. Other are just too busy for this approach. But no matter what camp you fall into, SYBEX has a book that can help you get the most out of your computer and computer software while learning at your own pace.

Beginners generally want to start at the beginning. The **ABC's** series, with its step-by-step lessons in plain language, helps you build basic skills quickly. Or you might try our **Quick & Easy** series, the friendly, full-color guide.

The **Mastering** and **Understanding** series will tell you everything you need to know about a subject. They're perfect for intermediate and advanced computer users, yet they don't make the mistake of leaving beginners behind.

If you're a busy person and are already comfortable with computers, you can choose from two SYBEX series—**Up & Running** and **Running Start**. The **Up & Running** series gets you started in just 20 lessons. Or you can get two books in one, a step-by-step tutorial and an alphabetical reference, with our **Running Start** series.

Everyone who uses computer software can also use a computer software reference. SYBEX offers the gamut—from portable **Instant References** to comprehensive **Encyclopedias, Desktop References**, and **Bibles**.

SYBEX even offers special titles on subjects that don't neatly fit a category—like **Tips & Tricks,** the **Shareware Treasure Chests,** and a wide range of books for Macintosh computers and software.

SYBEX books are written by authors who are expert in their subjects. In fact, many make their living as professionals, consultants or teachers in the field of computer software. And their manuscripts are thoroughly reviewed by our technical and editorial staff for accuracy and ease-of-use.

So when you want answers about computers or any popular software package, just help yourself to SYBEX.

For a complete catalog of our publications:

SYBEX Inc.
2021 Challenger Drive, Alameda, CA 94501
Tel: (415) 523-8233/(800) 227-2346 Telex: 336311
Fax: (415) 523-2373

Up & Running with DOS® 6

Second Edition

Alan Simpson

SYBEX ®

San Francisco • Paris • Düsseldorf • Soest

Acquisitions Editor: Dianne King
Series Editor: Joanne Cuthbertson
Editor: James A. Compton
Technical Editor: Linda Rose
Book Designer: Elke Hermanowski
Icon Designers: Helen Bruno and Suzanne Albertson
Screen Graphics: Cuong Le
Desktop Production Artist: Suzanne Albertson
Proofreader/Production Assistant: Kristin Amlie
Indexer: Ted Laux
Cover Designer: Archer Design

Screen reproductions produced with Collage Plus.

Collage Plus is a trademark of Inner Media.

SYBEX is a registered trademark of SYBEX Inc.

TRADEMARKS: SYBEX has attempted throughout this book to
distinguish proprietary trademarks from descriptive terms by following
the capitalization style used by the manufacturer. SYBEX is not
affiliated with any manufacturer.

Every effort has been made to supply complete and accurate
information. However, SYBEX assumes no responsibility for its use,
nor for any infringement of the intellectual property rights of third
parties which would result from such use.

First edition copyright ©1991

Library of Congress Card Number: 93-83902
ISBN: 0-7821-1258-7

Manufactured in the United States of America
10 9 8 7 6 5 4 3 2 1

SYBEX
Up & Running Books

The Up & Running series of books from SYBEX has been developed for committed, eager PC users who would like to become familiar with a wide variety of programs and operations as quickly as possible. We assume that you are comfortable with your PC and that you know the basic functions of word processing, spreadsheets, and database management. With this background, Up & Running books will show you in 20 steps what particular products can do and how to use them.

Who this book is for

Up & Running books are designed to save you time and money. First, you can avoid purchase mistakes by previewing products before you buy them—exploring their features, strengths, and limitations. Second, once you decide to purchase a product, you can learn its basics quickly by following the 20 steps—even if you are a beginner.

What this book provides

The first step usually covers software installation in relation to hardware requirements. You'll learn whether the program can operate with your available hardware as well as various methods for starting the program. The second step often introduces the program's user interface. The remaining 18 steps demonstrate the program's basic functions, using examples and short descriptions.

Contents & structure

 A clock shows the amount of time you can expect to spend at your computer for each step. Naturally, you'll need much less time if you only read through the step rather than complete it at your computer.

Special symbols and notes

You can also focus on particular points by scanning the short notes in the margins and locating the sections you are most interested in.

 At the beginning of each step, you'll see either one or two DOS version icons, indicating whether the techniques covered there are available only in DOS 6 or in both versions 5 and 6. These icons also appear as needed within steps.

In addition, three symbols highlight particular sections of text:

The Action symbol highlights important steps that you will carry out.

The Tip symbol indicates a practical hint or special technique.

The Warning symbol alerts you to a potential problem and suggestions for avoiding it.

We have structured the Up & Running books so that the busy user spends little time studying documentation and is not burdened with unnecessary text. An Up & Running book cannot, of course, replace a lengthier book that contains advanced applications. However, you will get the information you need to put the program to practical use and to learn its basic functions in the shortest possible time.

We welcome your comments

SYBEX is very interested in your reactions to the Up & Running series. Your opinions and suggestions will help all of our readers, including yourself. Please send your comments to: SYBEX Editorial Department, 2021 Challenger Drive, Alameda, CA 94501.

Preface

This book has two goals: First to help you learn DOS 6 quickly, easily, and painlessly. Second, to help you find answers to questions as they arise.

If you're new to DOS (perhaps coming over from a Macintosh or Unix system) or haven't used it in a while, you'll appreciate the first 7 steps, which will help you get oriented in a jiffy.

New DOS user

What's New in DOS 6?

If you're an experienced DOS user, you'll probably want to focus on what's new in DOS 6. Here's a quick overview of highlights, indicating which Step in this book describes the feature in more detail:

New features for everyone

- **DoubleSpace**: Lets you store twice as much information on your hard disk and floppies (Step 11).

- **MemMaker**: Makes efficient memory management as simple as typing a single command (Step 13).

- **Defrag**: Speeds up a sluggish hard disk (Step 12).

- **Easier Backup**: Offers better ways to back up your hard disk, from both DOS and Windows (Step 8).

- **Better Accident Recovery**: Windows and DOS versions of UNDELETE and UNFORMAT let you recover files that you've deleted accidentally (Step 9).

- **Virus Protection**: Windows and DOS versions of Microsoft Anti-Virus prevent, seek out, and destroy harmful viruses (Step 14).

- **Easy File Transfer**: You can connect two computers, transfer files easily between them, and share printers (Step 15).

- **Better Laptop Performance**: Get up to 25% more power from your laptop computer's battery (Step 16).

*Features
for More
Advanced
Users*

- **On-Line Documentation and Better Help:** Help is available from just about everywhere in DOS—including the command prompt (Steps 2 and 3).

- **Multiple Configurations:** You can define multiple configurations in a single CONFIG.SYS file, and choose a configuration at startup. For troubleshooting at startup, you can bypass selected CONFIG.SYS commands by pressing F8, or bypass CONFIG.SYS and AUTOEXEC.BAT altogether by pressing F5 (Step 18).

- **Smarter Batch Programs:** For DOS batch file programmers, the new CHOICE command presents a prompt to the user, and accepts input that you can later use in a decision (Step 19).

How to Use This Book

It's not necessary to read this book cover-to-cover. When you have a question or problem, take a look inside the front and back covers of this book for quick reminders and page numbers for common DOS tasks. If that doesn't help, try the Table of Contents up front, or the Index near the back of the book.

Table of Contents

DOS (rhymes with "floss") is an acronym for *D*isk *O*perating *S*ystem. On your computer, DOS gives you—and the programs you use—a means of filing, locating, and retrieving information stored on your disks. It's a required program, since your computer cannot get started without an operating system.

What Version of DOS Are You Using Now?

There are quite a few versions of DOS floating around, the latest and greatest being DOS 6. If DOS was installed when you bought your computer, you may not be sure exactly which version is currently installed. If you know how to start your computer and get to the DOS command prompt, you can follow these simple steps to find out:

Current version of DOS

1. Get to the DOS command prompt (usually A> or C> followed by a blinking cursor).

2. Type

    ver

    and press ↵.

You should see a message like *MS-DOS Version 6.00*. (Don't be concerned about the decimal portion of the version number.) Where you go from here depends on the currently installed version of DOS:

*   If the VER command shows that you are using MS-DOS Version 6, DOS 6 is already installed. You need not install it yourself. If you like, you can skip to Step 2 for an introduction to the DOS Shell.

*   If you are using Version 5 or earlier, continue reading below.

Should I Upgrade to DOS 6?

If you're not using DOS 6, you might want to consider upgrading after you read about what's new in the Preface of this book. If your main concern is "How much trouble is it to upgrade?" The quick answer is "Not much."

Is it a hassle to upgrade?

In general, installing DOS 6 is quick (about 15 to 30 minutes of your time), painless (it practically installs itself once you've gotten started), and risk-free (you can uninstall DOS 6 if you don't like the results).

For the remainder of this step, I'll assume you have DOS 6 in hand and have not installed it yet, but are ready to install it.

Before You Install DOS 6...

To avoid any problems during the installation procedure, it's best to ensure that no memory-resident disk-caching, anti-virus, or delete-protection programs are running when you start the installation.

Disabling memory-resident programs

If you're not sure how to do that, but do know a DOS expert, you may want to ask for some help. In a nutshell, though, you need to edit your CONFIG.SYS and AUTOEXEC.BAT files, and "comment out" any memory-resident virus, caching, and delete-protection programs. To comment out a command, put the word *rem* followed by a blank space in front of the command, as in the example below:

```
rem c:\dos\mirror.com
```

Changes you make to AUTOEXEC.BAT and CONFIG.SYS have absolutely no effect until the next time you start the computer. So be sure to save any changes to these files. Then reboot the computer (press Ctrl+Alt+Del or the reset button) before installing DOS 6.

Creating an Uninstall Disk

During the installation procedure, you'll be asked to insert an Uninstall disk in drive A. (This disk will safeguard your current information in case you cannot complete the installation successfully.) So before you begin installing, grab a new, blank floppy disk (it need not be formatted), and write DOS 6 UNINSTALL (or something like that) on the label.

If you're using 360K disks, you'll probably need two floppies. Label them UNINSTALL #1 and UNINSTALL #2.

Installing DOS 6 on a Hard Disk

You can install DOS 6 on your hard disk without erasing any files or reformatting. But if you have any important files on your hard disk, it's a good idea to back up everything before you get started. Just use your normal backup procedure (if you have one). Then, when you're ready to upgrade:

1. Start your computer as you normally do, and get to the DOS command prompt (typically C> or C:\>).

2. Insert the DOS 6 Setup disk in drive A or B.

3. If you put the Setup disk in drive A, type

    `a:setup`

    Or, if you put the Setup disk in drive B, type

    `b:setup`

4. Press ⏎.

5. Follow the installation instructions that appear on the screen.

Follow all of the instructions until you get to the screen informing you that you've successfully installed DOS 6. In the future, DOS will be loaded automatically each time you start your computer (you can use the VER command to verify).

Starting DOS 6

Once you've installed DOS 6 on your hard disk, starting it is as simple as turning on your computer:

1. Make sure all of your floppy disk drives are empty.

2. Turn on your computer (and monitor if it has a separate switch).

That's all there is to it. You can use the VER command described earlier to make sure you're using version 6. Then you can move on to Step 2.

Uninstalling DOS 6

When you install DOS 6 on a hard disk, the Setup program keeps a "safe" copy of your original system on the Uninstall disk.

If you cannot complete the installation, or find that DOS 6 just isn't working correctly on your computer, you can easily uninstall DOS 6 to return to your previous version. But do this *only* if you're sure you *don't* want to keep DOS 6 installed on your computer:

1. Insert the Uninstall disk that you created during the DOS 6 installation procedure into drive A.

2. Reboot (press Ctrl+Alt+Del or your computer's reset button).

3. Follow the instructions that appear on your screen.

Removing Your Previous DOS Version

If you use DOS 6 for a few days, and find that it's working just fine, you can recover some disk space by deleting your previous version of DOS. To do so:

1. Type

   deloldos

   at the DOS command prompt.

2. Press ↵.

DOS will delete the OLD_DOS.1 directory, as well as the DELOLDOS program. If you get the *Bad command or file name* error message when you try to run DELOLDOS, it's probably because somebody has already deleted the previous DOS version.

Step 2

Easy DOS It with the Shell

Starting the Shell

The DOS 6 Shell is the easiest way to get along with DOS. To start
the Shell from the DOS command prompt:

1. Type

    dosshell

    (notice the double *S*).

2. Press ↵.

Areas of the Shell

When the Shell first appears, it looks something like Figure 2.1. The
various areas of the Shell are summarized in Table 2.1.

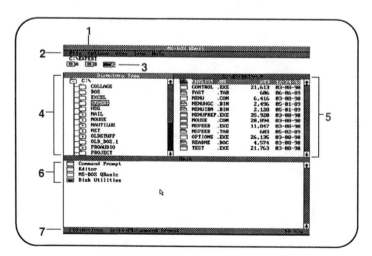

Figure 2.1: Areas of the DOS 6 Shell.

Number	Area/WindowName	Shows
1	Title Bar	Name of this program (MS-DOS Shell).
2	Menu Bar	Names of menus from which you can choose commands.
3	Drives Area	Disk drives available on your computer
4	Directory Tree	Directories on the current drive
5	Files List	Files on the current directory
6	Program List	Programs and groups of programs
7	Status Line	Available shortcut keys and current time

Table 2.1: Areas of the Shell

Using a Mouse in the Shell

Although you can use the DOS Shell with either the keyboard or a mouse, only a mouse makes using the Shell truly easy. This book uses the standard mouse terminology to describe mouse operations:

Mouse Pointer: (also called the *pointer*) Moves in whatever direction you roll the mouse.

Mouse Button: The active button on your mouse, typically the one that your index finger rests on naturally.

Click: Position the mouse pointer, then press and immediately release the mouse button.

Double-Click: Position the mouse pointer, then click the mouse button twice as quickly as you can—so there is no time lag between the two clicks.

Drag: Position the mouse pointer, then hold down the mouse button while rolling the mouse. When the mouse pointer gets to your desired destination, *then* you can release the mouse button.

What the Shell Is Showing You

The Shell is most useful for showing how the information on your computer is organized:

- **Drives**: The Drives Area shows available disk drives. Your computer might have one or two diskette drives, named A and B, as well as a hard disk drive named C. It might also have additional network, CD-ROM, or other drives, named D, E, and so on up to Z.

- **Directory**: The Directory Tree area shows the names of directories (also called subdirectories) on the currently selected drive. If you think of a drive as a filing cabinet, each directory is like a single drawer in that cabinet, with its own unique set of files.

- **File**: The Files List area shows only the names of files on the currently selected directory. A file is the computer equivalent of a manila folder file in a file cabinet.

As you'll learn, a large part of using your computer effectively is simply knowing how to get to a file by choosing its drive, directory, and file name.

Getting Around In the Shell

If you have a mouse, you can move the mouse pointer to any area of the Shell, then click the mouse button to move the highlighter into that area. You can also select any specific item in the Shell, such as a directory name, simply by clicking that name.

Mouse

You can also use the Tab and Shift+Tab keys to move from one area of the Shell to the next. Once the highlighter gets to the area you want, you can use the →, ←, ↑, and ↓ keys, as appropriate, to move the highlighter within that area.

←, →, and Other Special Keys

Num Lock Key

If the ↑, ↓, →, ←, PgUp, PgDn, and other special keys are combined with the numbers on your numeric keypad, those keys will work *only* when the Num Lock key is turned off.

Undoing Your Last Move

Whoops!

If you find yourself in unfamiliar territory while exploring the Shell, and you want to back out to more familiar territory, press the Escape key (Esc).

Using Scroll Bars

If an area (or "window") in the Shell contains more items than can fit in that window, you can use the scroll bar to scroll through items that are currently out of view. For instance, Figure 2.2 shows the scroll bar next to the Files List window.

The scroll bar works only when its window contains more items than are currently visible. To use a scroll bar:

Mouse

- To scroll up or down one line, click one of the scroll arrows at the top or bottom of the scroll bar.

- To scroll continuously, move the mouse pointer to one of the scroll arrows, and hold down the left mouse button.

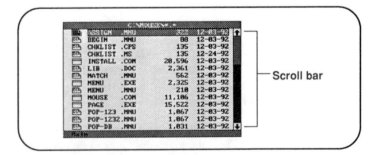

Figure 2.2: Scroll bar next to Files List.

- To scroll to a particular part of the list, drag the scroll box
  (the white or lighter portion of the scroll bar) to the approximate location that you want to view.

In some cases, you can quickly jump to a section of the list by typing
a letter.

To use the scroll bars with the keyboard, first use the Tab or   *Keyboard*
Shift+Tab keys to move the cursor anywhere within the window that
has the scroll bar attached to it. Then:

- To scroll up or down a line, press the ↑ or ↓ key.

- To scroll continuously, hold down the ↓ or ↑ key.

- To jump to the top of the list, press Ctrl+Home (or just
  Home on a vertical list).

- To scroll to the end of the list, press Ctrl+End (or just End
  on a vertical list).

Using the Menus

The menu bar near the top of the Shell gives you options (also called
commands) for getting things done in the Shell. When you choose a
command from the menu bar, a menu opens, as in Figure 2.3.

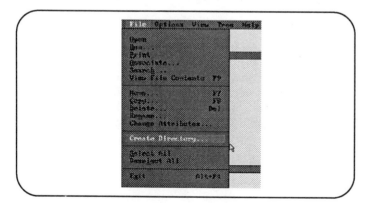

Figure 2.3: The File menu opened in the Shell.

Mouse

Keyboard

You can use either the mouse or the keyboard to choose commands from the menu bar and menus.

To choose commands from menus using the mouse, simply click whatever option you want.

To choose menu commands with a keyboard, press and release the Alt or F10 key to move the highlighter into the menu bar. Then,

- Type the underlined letter for the command you want to select.
- Or, use the ←, →, ↑, ↓ keys to move the highlighter to the option you want, then press ↵ to select that option.

How This Book Shows Menu Sequences

*The ⇒
symbol*

Many actions in the Shell require that you select a series of commands from the menus. This book uses the ⇒ symbol to show a series of menu selections, as in this example:

Choose Options ⇒ File Display Options

This is just a shorthand way of saying "Choose Options from the menu bar, then choose File Display Options from the pull-down menu that appears." You can use either your mouse or the keyboard to make those menu selections.

Dimmed, Unavailable Commands

When you open a menu, some commands may be dimmed. Those commands are not relevant at the moment, and therefore cannot be selected. For example, many options on the File menu will be dimmed and unavailable until you select one or more file names from the files list, as described a little later.

Using Shortcut Keys

Many menu commands in the Shell include a shortcut key, or key combination, that you can use instead of going through the menus. For example, F7, F8, and Del (Delete) are shortcut keys for the Move, Copy, and Delete commands on the File menu shown earlier.

Some shortcuts are actually keystroke combinations, represented as *key+key*. This combination means to hold down the first key as you tap the second key. For example, the instruction to *Press Alt+F1* means "Hold down the Alt key, tap the F1 key, then release the Alt key."

Key+Key Combinations

Using Dialog Boxes

Some commands that you choose from the menus will request additional information via a *dialog box*. For example, selecting Options ⇒ File Display Options opens the dialog box shown in Figure 2.4. Let's look at this example.

Moving Within a Dialog Box

When a dialog box is displayed, you can move the cursor to various options and make selections. The current option contains the cursor, and may also be surrounded by a dotted line.

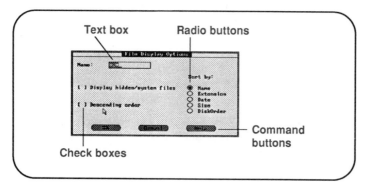

Figure 2.4: A sample dialog box.

Mouse

To move to a different option in the dialog box with a mouse, click the option or area you want to move to.

Keyboard

With a keyboard:

1. Press Tab to move down (or to the right), or Shift+Tab to move in the opposite direction.
2. Within a set of options (such as the radio buttons under Sort By in Figure 2.4), use the ↑, ↓, ←, and → keys to move the cursor in the direction you want to go.

Entering and Changing Text

Some dialog boxes request that you type text into a rectangular box within the dialog box, such as the box next to the Name: option in the illustration. To use such a text box:

1. Move the cursor into the box either by clicking the box with a mouse, or by pressing Tab (or Shift+Tab).

   With a mouse, you can click the exact *insertion point* where you want to start typing.

2. To replace the contents of the box completely, just start typing your new text.
3. To change the existing contents of the box, first move the cursor using your mouse or the arrow keys, then start typing.
4. To delete specific characters, position the cursor to the character you want to delete, and then press Backspace or Delete (Del).
5. To leave the completed box, click another area with your mouse, or press Tab or Shift+Tab.

Filling Check Boxes

Many dialog boxes also have *check boxes,* for options that you can turn on or off. An X in the box indicates the option is on; an empty box indicates it is off.

To activate (put an X into) a check box, or deactivate (remove the X from) a check box with a mouse, click the check box.

Mouse

Or, if you are using the keyboard:

1. Position the cursor to the box with the Tab or Shift+Tab keys.

Keyboard

2. Press the space bar, or ↵.

Using Option Buttons

Option buttons (also called "radio buttons") in a dialog box work like the buttons used to select a station on a car radio; pressing a button automatically "unpresses" another button (since you can't listen to two radio stations at once). The technique for using radio buttons is similar to that for using check boxes.

With a mouse, click the option you want.

Mouse

On the keyboard,

1. Use the Tab or Shift+Tab keys to move to the general area of the radio buttons.

Keyboard

2. Use the ↑ and ↓ keys to move to the button you want.

Using Command Buttons

Command buttons are usually listed along the bottom of a dialog box. To choose a command button:

Click the button you want, or

Mouse

Keyboard   Press Tab or Shift+Tab until the cursor lands on the button you want. Then press ↵ to choose that button.

Saving/Canceling Dialog Box Changes

Most dialog boxes have a set of command buttons that you can use as follows:

- To save whatever selections you made in the dialog box and return to where you came from, choose OK.

- To leave the dialog box without saving your selections or changes, choose Cancel (or press Esc).

- To get help with this dialog box, click the Help command button (if one is available) or press F1.

Improving Your View

You can use commands from the menus to change the appearance of the Shell to your liking.

Changing Screen Colors

To change the screen colors displayed by the Shell:

1. Choose Options ⇒ Colors.
2. Highlight the name of any color scheme, and choose Preview. Repeat this step until you find a color scheme you like.
3. Choose OK.

Changing the Text/Graphics Appearance

Depending on your monitor, you can choose from among several screen resolutions in graphics or text mode:

1. Choose Options ⇒ Display.

2. Highlight the name of any available display mode, then choose Preview. Repeat this step until you find a mode you like.

3. Choose OK.

Changing the View

You also have some control over which areas appear in the Shell. First choose View, then one of the options described below:

- **Single File List:** Hides the Program List area.

- **Dual File List:** Displays two independent Drive, Directory Tree, and File List areas.

- **All Files:** Displays all the files on the current drive. Information about the currently highlighted file name appears where the Directory Tree normally appears.

- **Program/File Lists:** The standard view.

- **Program List:** Shows only the Program List window.

Getting Help in the Shell

DOS 6 (like DOS 5 before it) provides useful, accessible help on your screen. Learning to use the built-in help system can be a great timesaver in finding new (or forgotten) information without referring to written documentation. Whenever you're in the Shell, you can get help using any of these methods:

- Press the F1 key.

- If you're in a dialog box that has a Help button, click that button with your mouse.

- Choose Help from the menu bar, and then choose an option from the Help menu that opens.

Help will appear on the screen in a help window. With the first two methods, you'll see information about the command you've selected or the current dialog box; this is known as *context-sensitive* help. Choosing Help from the menu bar displays a pull-down menu that offers different ways of using the help system.

Learning to Use Help

Probably the best way to learn to use the help system is by doing. Choose Help from the menu bar, then choose Using Help from the pull-down menu that appears. Then, as you'll learn, you can use the scroll bar or the ↑, ↓, PgUp and PgDn keys to scroll through and read additional text.

Within the help window, you can get information on any colored topic. Just double-click the topic, or press Tab or Shift+Tab until the topic you want is highlighted, then press ↵.

Exiting Help

When you've finished with the help window, click the Close button or press Escape.

Exiting the Shell

To leave the Shell:

- Choose File ⇒ Exit (or press Alt+F4)

You'll see the command prompt (C>), which offers another way to interact with DOS.

As an alternative to using the DOS Shell, DOS 6 offers the command line—which was the only interface that DOS versions 3 and earlier offered. The command line gives you access to many features of DOS 6 that aren't available through the Shell.

Getting to the Command Prompt

In most cases, the DOS command prompt appears automatically when you start your computer. If you are in some other program, such as the DOS Shell or Windows, you'll be returned to the command prompt after you *exit* that program. As we'll discuss in Step 5, different programs require different techniques to exit. However, pressing Alt+F4 and choosing File ⇒ Exit from the menu bar are two common exit techniques.

The Command Prompt

The command prompt usually consists of nothing more than the current drive and directory name followed by a greater-than sign and a blinking cursor. For example, C:\> when you're on hard disk drive C, or A:\> when you're on floppy disk drive A.

Entering a Command

A command is simply an instruction that tells DOS what to do. Entering a command always involves two basic steps:

1. Type the complete command. If necessary, use the Backspace key to make corrections.

2. To tell the computer to carry out the command, press ↵.

Upper/lowercase in Commands

DOS is oblivious to upper/lowercase distinctions, so you can use whatever case you want when typing commands. For example, as far as DOS is concerned:

```
DIR A: /W
dir a: /w
Dir A: /W
```

are all the same thing.

Making Corrections

If you make a mistake while typing a command, and notice it before pressing ↵, you can use the Backspace or ← key to back up and make corrections. Optionally, if you type a command and notice a mistake (before pressing ↵), and just want to start over, you can press Escape (Esc), then ↵, to get to a new command prompt.

Canceling Commands

If you type a command, press ↵, and then realize you've made a mistake, or for some other reason want to terminate the command altogether, you can press Ctrl+Break or Ctrl+C.

Note that this only cancels a command that is in progress. If the command has already completed its task, pressing Ctrl+C or Ctrl+Break has no effect.

Commonly Used Commands

The trick to using commands, of course, is knowing which command you need, and how to type it. You'll learn about specific commands in the upcoming steps. For quick reference, I've also listed some common DOS operations, and the page numbers where you'll find how to perform those operations, in the inside front covers of this book.

Knowing how to type a command, once you've figured out which command you need, is a matter of using the correct syntax for the command. You can use the online documentation or summary help to get this information, as needed, right on your screen.

A Manual on Your Screen

DOS 6 comes with complete online documentation—sort of a manual-on-disk. To get to the online documentation, enter the command **help** at the command prompt (don't forget to press ↵). You'll be taken to MS-DOS Command Reference. To use the command reference:

- Click any *jump* (text between the < and > angle brackets) to jump to that topic or command.

Mouse

- Or, type the first letter of a jump, or use the Tab, Shift+Tab, ↑, ↓, PgUp, and PgDn keys to move the cursor to a jump, then press ↵ to select it.

Keyboard

Depending on the command or topic you've chosen, you can also

- Choose <Notes> for more information.

- Press F1 or choose Help ⇒ How To Use MS-DOS Help for additional help.

- Choose <Examples> to see examples of the command.

- Choose <Syntax> to return to the first help page.

- Press (or click) Alt+C to return to the Table of Contents.

- Press (or click) Alt+N to move to the next page (if any).

- Press (or click) Alt+B to move back to the previous page (if any).

- Choose File ⇒ Print to print the current help information.

- Choose File ⇒ Exit when you're ready to leave the online documentation.

If you're at the DOS command prompt, and want to look at the online documentation for a particular command, just type **help** followed by a space and the command you want help with. For example, entering the command **help dir** will take you straight to the online documentation for the DIR command.

Getting Summary Help

The one problem with the online documentation is that you need to exit it to get back to the command prompt before you type in a command. At which time, the syntax is erased from the screen!

When you just need a brief reminder of the purpose or syntax of a command, you can use the abbreviated help. Just type the command you need help with, followed by a space and /?. For example, entering the command **dir** /? displays the abbreviated help for the DIR command. The command prompt reappears as well, so that help is visible as you type your command.

If you want to see a list of all the DOS commands with brief descriptions, enter the new DOS 6 command **doshelp**, then press any key to scroll from one screen to the next.

What the Help Is Telling You

At first glance, the "help" that appears on the screen may look like a secret message from an alien planet. But it's really telling you about the purpose of the command, as well as its syntax. The syntax of a command usually looks something like this:

```
command parameter(s) switch(es)
```

Command Syntax

Optional parameters and switches are shown in brackets; you can exclude them if you wish. For example, if you enter **dir** /? to look up the syntax for the DIR command, you'll see something like this:

```
DIR [drive:] [path] [filename] [/P] [/W]
[/A[[:]attribs]] [/O[[:]sortord]] [/S] [/B]
[/L] [/C[H]]
```

In this example, every parameter and switch is optional, and therefore shown in brackets.

Note that the brackets are used in the syntax display to indicate optional parameters and switches only. You never include the brackets when typing a command.

In addition to the syntax, the help screen displays information describing the purpose of each parameter and switch in the command's syntax.

Parameters

A parameter generally tells DOS what disk drive, directory, and or file(s) you want to work on. In many cases, if you omit the parameter, DOS assumes that you are referring to the current drive and directory. For example, the command **dir** lists all the files on the current drive and directory.

If you do use a parameter, it should follow the command, and be separated from the command by a space (like two words in a sentence). For example, the command **dir c:\dos** tells DOS to list the names of the files on the directory named DOS on drive C.

When specifying a drive, directory, and file name in a command, you separate each with a backslash (\), and *never* include a blank space.

Drivers, directories, file names, and wildcards

In the file name, you can use these two wildcards:

- A ? stands for any single character
- An * stands for any sequence of characters

Thus, when you want to refer to "all the files that end with .EXE, that are on the DOS directory of drive C," you'd type the parameter as **c:\dos*.exe** as in the example below, where the parameter is used with the DIR command:

```
dir c:\dos\*.exe
```

Switches

Many commands also allow you to use optional switches, which further refine how the command operates. A switch is generally a forward slash (/) followed by a single letter or word. Switches are usually placed as the last items in a command, but they can appear in any order. Each should be preceded by a blank space.

As an example, the DIR command provides a /w switch, which widens the list of filenames it displays into multiple columns across the screen. To see a wide display of the files on the current drive and directory, you would enter

```
dir /w
```

To use the /w switch with the command *and* a parameter, you'd enter:

```
dir c:\dos /w
```

Errors in Commands

When you type a command incorrectly, you'll see an error message, such as *Invalid switch* or *Bad command or file name*. When that happens, you might want to look at the Examples and Notes in the online documentation for additional information, or check Step 20 of this book for more information. Then re-enter the command correctly.

Repeating a Command

If you need to repeat the same command, or a portion of the same command, several times, you need not retype it from scratch each time. Instead, DOS allows you to retrieve all, or any part of, the preceding command using the keys shown in Table 3.1 at the command prompt (after you've entered at least one command).

Key	Effect
F1 (or →)	Recalls one character.
F3	Recalls the entire previous command.
Backspace (or ←)	Deletes the character to the left of the cursor, and also moves back a character.
Insert (Ins)	Inserts the next characters you type at the current cursor position.
F2	Copies characters up to, but not including the next character you type.
F4	Skips characters in the previous command, up to but not including the next character you type.

Table 3.1: Keys Used to Copy Characters from the Previous Command

Using DOSKEY to Repeat Commands

DOS includes a separate program named DOSKEY that gives you added flexibility in recalling previous commands. You can start DOSKEY at any time simply by entering the command **doskey** at the command prompt. Better yet, to have DOSKEY's abilities readily available at all times, your best bet would be to add the command to your AUTOEXEC.BAT file. (You'll learn about AUTOEXEC.BAT in Steps 17 and 19.)

Once DOSKEY is loaded, you can use the ↑, ↓, PgUp, and PgDn keys to scroll through commands. Additional keys and techniques are listed in the Notes section of the online documentation.

Pausing and Printing Screen Text

Some commands, like DIR, display long lists of text that whiz by on the screen pretty quickly. You can stop scrolling text at any time by pressing Ctrl+S or the Pause key (if your keyboard has one). To resume scrolling, press any key.

As an alternative, you can put | **more** at the end of the command to pause after every screenful of information. Or you can put **>prn** at the end of the command to send its output to the printer. See Step 10 for more information about printing.

One of the most important skills in using your computer effectively is finding files when you need them. Sometimes, you may not remember where a particular file is, and therefore may need to "look around" to find it. At other times, such as when you are installing a new program, the user's manual will tell you to go to a particular drive and directory to install or run the program.

Selecting a Drive in the Shell

To locate a particular file, you first need to get to the appropriate disk drive. To do so from the DOS Shell, use the method that's best for you:

- Click the drive's icon or name in the Drives Area of the Shell (just below the menu bar).

Mouse

Or, from the keyboard

1. Press Tab until you've highlighted the Drives Area of the shell.

2. Press ← and/or → until the drive you want is highlighted, then press ↵.

Keyboard

The name of the current disk drive remains highlighted in the Drives Area of the Shell, and also appears near the top of the Directory Tree and Files Area of the Shell.

If you attempt to switch to a floppy disk drive that is empty, or contains a faulty or unformatted disk, you'll see the message *Drive not ready* (or something similar) and the options to try the operation again or cancel it. To try again, insert (or replace) the disk and click OK or press ↵. To cancel, click Cancel or press Escape (Esc).

Selecting a Drive at the Command Prompt

If you're at the command prompt and want to switch to another drive, enter the drive name followed by a colon (:). For example, to switch to drive A you would enter

    a:

To switch back to drive C, you'd enter

    c:

Selecting a Directory in the Shell

Every disk contains at least one directory, called the *root directory*, which is named \. When you switch to a drive, its root directory name and icon are automatically displayed near the top of the Directory Tree, and the names of any additional directories on that disk are displayed beneath the root directory icon.

To switch to a different directory on the current disk drive:

Mouse

* Click the name of the directory you want to switch to.

Or, on the keyboard

Keyboard

1. Press Tab until the Directory Tree is highlighted.
2. Use the arrow keys to highlight the directory you want.

The Files area shows the names of files on the currently selected directory.

Expanding the Directory Tree

To avoid clutter on the screen, the Directory Tree displays only the first directory level beneath the root. To explore the directories on a disk thoroughly, you need to be able to expand (and collapse) the number of levels shown.

Expanding One Branch One Level

A plus sign (+) within a directory icon means you can expand that branch by at least one level. To expand a single directory level to view the names of any subdirectories beneath it:

- Click the icon (containing a plus sign) for the directory. *Mouse*

Or, if you're using a keyboard

1. Use the arrow keys to highlight the name of the directory you want. *Keyboard*
2. Press the + key, or select Tree ⇒ Expand One Level.

Expanding One Branch Fully

A branch of the Directory Tree may have several subdirectory levels. Rather than expanding the branch out one level at a time, you can fully expand it by following these steps:

1. Select the directory that you want to fully expand. *Keyboard*
2. Press the asterisk (*) key, or select Tree ⇒ Expand Branch.

Fully Expanding All Branches

To see all the branches of the directory fully expanded,

- Press Ctrl+* or select Tree ⇒ Expand All. *Keyboard*

To get some practice with these techniques, you should try experimenting with the disks and directories on your computer. Table 4.1 lists some additional optional shortcut keys that you can use to move through the Directory Tree.

Key	Effect
Home	Selects the root directory
End	Selects the directory at the bottom of the tree.
↑	Selects the directory listed above the current directory.
↓	Selects the directory listed below the current directory.
First-letter	Moves to the directory name that begins with that letter.

Table 4.1: Optional Keys Used in the Directory Tree.

Collapsing Directory Levels

A minus sign (–) in a directory name's icon indicates that the branch can be collapsed, in case you want to unclutter the Directory Tree area. Here's how to collapse a branch:

Mouse

- Click the icon (containing a minus sign) for the branch that you want to collapse.

Or

Keyboard

1. Move the highlighter to the branch you want to collapse.

2. Press the minus key (–) or select Tree ⇒ Collapse Branch from the pull-down menu.

To collapse the directory tree back to one level, first collapse the root (uppermost) directory, then expand it again.

If the directory tree does not fit within the Directory Tree area of the screen, you can also use the scroll bar at the right of the window to scroll up and down.

Selecting a Directory at the Command Prompt

If you're at the command prompt and don't want to switch to the Shell, you can use the CHDIR command, or the abbreviated version CD, to switch to a different directory. For example, entering the command

    cd \dos

would take you to the DOS directory (if it exists) on the current drive. The command

    cd \

would take you to the root directory of the current drive.

Viewing Directory Names at the Prompt

You can use the TREE command at the DOS command prompt to view the names of directories on the current drive. The command

    tree

shows the names of directories beneath the current directory only. The command

    tree \

displays the names of *all* directories on the current drive. The command

    tree \ >prn

prints the directory list. You'll probably need to eject the printed page from the printer to see it, as discussed in Step 10.

For more information and examples of the CHDIR and TREE commands, use the online documentation as discussed in Step 3.

Displaying File Names in the Shell

In the Shell, the Files Area to the right of the Directory Tree displays the names of the files on the currently selected drive and directory (or subdirectory). It also shows the size of each file, and the date that the file was created or last changed.

Viewing Selected File Names

A file name can contain up to eight letters, and may include an extension up to three characters in length. When displaying file names, you can use two wildcard characters to isolate certain file names:

- ? Matches any single character in a file name

- * Matches any group of characters in a file name

Initially, DOS uses *.* (which you can see at the top of the Files Area window). This pattern matches any file name followed by any extension—that is, every file name on the directory.

To display only file names that match a particular pattern:

1. Select the drive and directory that contain the files you want to view.

2. Select Options ⇒ File Display Options.

3. Type in the pattern for the file names that you want to view.

4. Press ↵ (or Esc if you change your mind).

The Files Area will only display file names that match your pattern, even if you switch to another directory. With experience, you'll find that this is particularly helpful if you remember to use consistency when naming the files you create. For example, if you store weekly data in separate files, and name those files WEEK1.DAT, WEEK2.DAT, and so forth, you can easily isolate those file names with the pattern WEEK*.DAT, which in turn makes it easier to move, copy, or delete them as a group in the future, if necessary.

Remember to change the pattern back to *.* when you want to see all tiles in each directory again.

Sorting File Names

The file names in the Files Area are initially presented in alphabetical order by first name. Sometimes, however, another sort order might be handy. Suppose you can't remember what name you gave to a file, but do remember the approximate data you created or changed it. You could display the file names sorted in data order, so that all the files in each directory would be grouped together by date.

To change the Files List arrangement:

1. Select the drive and directory that contain the file names you want to view.

2. Select Options ⇒ File Display Options.

3. Optionally, type in a file name or pattern (with or without wildcard characters).

4. Select options from the dialog box, as described below:

    Name: Alphabetical order by file name (the default order).

    Extension: Alphabetical order by extension.

    Date: Chronological order by the date created or last changed.

    Size: Largest to smallest size

    DiskOrder: Order in which file was placed on the disk.

    Display Hidden/System files: If selected, the Files List will include the names of any normally hidden and system files.

    Descending Order: If selected, displays the file names in reverse sort order, such as Z to A alphabetically, or latest to earliest date, or largest to smallest file.

5. Click OK or press ↵.

Viewing File Names
at the Command Prompt

If you're at the command prompt and want to view file names without going into the Shell, use the DIR command. For example, the command

```
dir
```

lists the names of all files on the current directory. You can scroll through the display one page at a time by using the /p switch, like this:

```
dir /p
```

As with most commands, you can use wildcards to view particular types of files. For example, this command displays only files that have the extension .EXE:

```
dir *.exe /p
```

Use the /o switch followed by a letter to display names in a particular order. For example, this command prints a list of file names in alphabetical order:

```
dir /on >prn
```

For more information on the DIR command, see the online documentation, or enter **dir** /? as discussed in Step 3.

Step 5

Running Programs

15

Most people buy computers to run "application" programs, such as word processors and spreadsheets. DOS provides several techniques for starting programs; the alternative you choose is pretty much up to you.

About Programs

All programs are stored on disk in *program files* (also called *executable* files). The file name of a program file always has one of the following extensions: .EXE, .COM or .BAT. The file name of the program is also the command you use to start the program. For example, the command to run a program named WP.EXE (or WP.COM, or WP.BAT) is WP.

In addition to the main executable files, a large program may have overlay, resource, and other supporting files. All of these are controlled automatically by the main program file; you don't work with them directly. The directory that contains the program file and any supporting files is called that program's *home directory.*

Starting a Program from the Command Prompt

To start a program from the DOS command prompt, you need to know the program's startup command, as shown in its documentation. Startup commands for some popular programs are listed in Table 5.1. Once you know the program's startup command, all you need to do to run that program is:

1. Type the program's startup command.

2. Press ↵.

Program Nane	Startup Command	To Exit
dBASE III Plus	dBASE	Setup ⇒ Quit
dBASE IV	dBASE	Exit ⇒ Quit
Excel for Windows	win excel	Alt+F4 (twice)
Lotus 1-2-3	123	/QY
Paradox	paradox	Exit ⇒ Yes
Quattro Pro (DOS)	Q	File ⇒ Exit
Windows	win	Alt+F4
Word for Windows	win winword	Alt+F4 (twice)
WordPerfect (DOS)	wp	F7
WordPerfect for Windows	win wpwin	Alt+F4 (twice)

Table 5.1: Startup and Exit Commands for Several Popular Programs

If you get an error message, such as *Bad command or file name,* when you try to start a program, one of three things is wrong:

- You typed the command incorrectly; simply retype it.

- Or, you cannot run the program from the current drive and directory because its home directory is not included in the current PATH setting (discussed in Step 17). Switch to the program's home directory and try again. Or try running the program from the Files List in the Shell.

- Or, you're trying to run a program that's never been in-stalled on your hard disk. Install the program according to the instructions in its documentation.

Exiting a Program

Once you start a program, it stays in control until you exit.

In addition to startup commands, Table 5.1 includes the exit commands for the programs listed. Notice that for Windows programs you press Alt+F4 twice—first to exit to Windows (from which you can run other programs if you like), and again to return to DOS. Exit commands that contain ⇒ indicate selections you make from menus.

Alt+F4 (twice)

Upon exiting, you may be asked if you want to save your work. You should choose Yes, then enter a file name (up to eight characters, no spaces or punctuation), press ↵, and follow any additional instructions to return to DOS or Windows.

Starting a Program from the DOS Shell Files List

If you're in the Shell, you can start a program by selecting its name in the Files List. To do so, you need to know the exact location and name of the program file. You can use either a mouse, or your keyboard, to make the appropriate selections:

1. In the Disk Drives Area, select the disk drive on which the program is stored.

2. In the Directory Tree, select the directory that holds the program.

3. In the Files Area, double-click the program's file name, or highlight its name and press ↵. (Remember—the file name must have the extension .EXE, .COM, or .BAT.)

When you exit the program, you'll be returned to the Shell.

Starting a Program with the Shell's Run Command

You can also start a program in the Shell using the File menu:

1. Select File ⇒ Run.

2. In the dialog box, type the program's startup command and any optional parameters that the program accepts (as described in its documentation).

3. Click OK, or press ↵.

If the requested program is not accessible from the current directory, you'll receive the *Bad command or file name* message, as when you try to run an inaccessible program from the command prompt. Try using the Files List to locate and start the program.

Associating Files with Programs

Yet another method of running programs is to set up an *association* between the program and the files that you create and change with that program. This allows you to start a program just by opening an associated file.

Some applications assign a file name extension automatically when you save a file. Others, such as Wordperfect, do not. Suppose you use the extension .WP for your Wordperfect files. If you associate that extension with the program, double-clicking any .WP file name will instruct DOS to load WordPerfect along with the file you selected. Quite convenient!

To set up an association between a file name extension and a program:

1. Go to any directory that has at least one file of the type you want to associate with a program.

2. In the Files List area, select a file name with the appropriate extension, either by clicking it once, or by moving the highlighter to the file name using the arrow keys.

3. Select File ⇒ Associate.

4. If the program's home directory is not in the current PATH setting (see Step 17), type the complete home directory specification and the program command (for example, **C:\WP51\WP**). If the program's home directory is in the PATH, you can just type the program's command or file name (**WP.EXE** or **WP**).

5. Click OK or press ↵.

To test the results, double-click any file with the appropriate extension (or highlight it and press ↵). If a problem arises, keep in mind the following, and make corrections as necessary:

- The file extension you associate with a program must be one the program can load automatically. Refer to that program's documentation for details.

- You can associate up to 20 extensions with one program. For example, you could associate .WP, .LET, .TXT and others with your favorite word processing program. However, you cannot associate an extension with more than one program. For example, you cannot associate the .WP extension with more than one word processor.

- If the associated files are likely to be stored on several directories, it's best to have the program's home directory listed in the current PATH setting.

Temporarily Bypassing an Association

Suppose you set up an association between an extension like .WP and your favorite word processor, but then later want to use a different program (perhaps a desktop publishing program) to work with one of your .WP files.

You need not go to any lengths to disassociate the .WP file and the word processor. Instead, just run the desktop publishing program on its own (perhaps using File ⇒ Run). Once that program is running, use its File ⇒ Open (or File ⇒ Import) commands to pull in a copy of the .WP file.

Terminating an Association

If you want to terminate the association between a program and a file name extension:

1. Select any file in the Files area that has the extension you want to disassociate.

2. Select File ⇒ Associate.

3. Press Backspace to erase the association.

4. Click on OK, or press ⏎.

Running Programs from the Program List

A fourth means of running a program is the Program List near the bottom of the screen. In DOS's off-the-shelf configuration, that list contains only a handful of program options in the Main group, and a few options grouped together in a group called Disk Utilities. (If you share a computer, another user may have added more programs and program groups to the list.) To run one of those programs:

Mouse

1. If the name of the program that you want to run is not displayed, select the group that contains that program by double-clicking the group name.

2. Double-click the name of the program you want to run.

If you are using a keyboard:

Keyboard

1. Press Tab to bring the highlighter to the Program List area near the bottom of the screen.

2. Highlight the name of the group (if any) that contains the program you want to run, then press ⏎ to select that group.

3. Highlight the name of the program you want to run, and press ⏎.

Running Multiple Programs

DOS 6 includes a *task swapper*, which makes it easy to switch from one program to another without going through the time-consuming step of exiting and reloading programs.

Activating the Task Swapper

To run multiple programs, you must first activate the task swapper:

- Select Options ⇒ Enable Task Swapper.

A new window with the heading Active Task List is added to the lower right corner of the Shell screen. Also, the Enable Task Swapper option on the Options pull-down menu has a diamond next to it, since that feature is now enabled and active.

Adding a Program to the Active Task List

To add a program to the task list:

1. Use any of the techniques described above to run the program of your choosing.

2. To return to the Shell, press Alt+Tab (or if that doesn't work, try Alt+Esc or Ctrl+Esc).

The name of the program you've left now appears in the Active Task List. You can repeat steps 1 and 2 to run as many programs as you wish.

Switching Among Tasks

After starting one or more tasks in the Active Task List, you can easily move among them:

- In the Active Task List area, double click the name of the program you want to switch to.

Mouse

Or, if you're using the keyboard:

1. Press Tab until you've highlighted the Active Task List area.

2. Use the ↑ and/or ↓ keys to highlight the name of the program you want to switch to.

3. Press ↵.

As a shortcut, you can switch back to the program that you left most recently just by pressing Alt+Tab again. Or you can hold down the Alt key and press Tab repeatedly to cycle through current tasks. You'll see the name of the current task near the top of the screen. When you see the name of the task you want to switch to, release the Alt key.

Keep in mind that DOS doesn't *run* all the programs in the Active Task List simultaneously. The moment you press Alt+Tab to leave a program and return to the Shell, that program goes into a state of suspension, and does not resume its activities until you return to it.

Terminating a Task Normally

To terminate a task, thereby removing it from the Active Task List:

1. Go to the program that you want to terminate.

2. Exit that program in the usual manner (that is, according to its documentation).

Before turning off your computer, you should terminate all programs in the Active Task List to prevent potential loss of data. If you make a habit of always attempting to exit the Shell with the File ⇒ Exit option before you turn off the computer, you'll be less likely to turn off the computer while tasks are still running. In fact, the Shell's File ⇒ Exit command won't let you exit the Shell while programs are active in the Active Task List.

Recovering from Abnormal Program Failure

If a program in the Active Task List crashes, and you cannot terminate it normally, you can remove it from the Active Task List by following these steps:

1. Go to the Active Task List in the Shell.

2. Highlight the name of the program you want to terminate.

3. Select File ⇒ Delete, or press the Delete (Del) key.

The screen will remind you that you should use this technique only as a last resort to terminate a program. If this is your last resort, select OK. Because the stability of DOS is now compromised (that is, DOS may not be working correctly), you should next try to terminate all other programs in the Task List normally. Then leave the Shell by selecting File ⇒ Exit. Finally, reboot the system by pressing Ctrl+Alt+Del. That will restart DOS from scratch and bring it back to normal.

Temporary Exit to DOS

If you need to get to the command prompt while you have programs running in the Task Swapper, you can do either of the following:

- Press Shift+F9.

- Or choose Command Prompt from the Program List near the bottom-left corner of the screen.

This kind of exit is sometimes referred to as a *temporary exit* or *suspended exit* because a copy of the Shell (and any other programs) remains in memory. To return to the program from which you made the temporary exit:

1. Type **exit** at the DOS command prompt.

2. Press ↵.

The Safest Time to Turn off Your Computer

If you turn off your computer without closing all files and programs first, you may *corrupt* any files that you have open at the moment, thereby losing some of your work. To avoid this problem, make a habit of taking the following steps just before you turn off your computer:

1. Make sure you're at the DOS command prompt.

2. Type **exit** and press ↵. Then...

    - If you just see the DOS command prompt again, no programs are running. It's safe to turn off your computer.

    - If you're returned to the Shell or some other program, exit that program to return to DOS, and repeat steps 1 and 2.

Step 6

Copying and Deleting

This step presents techniques for "general housekeeping" on your computer. I'll focus on the Shell, where these jobs are easiest to perform. But I'll also refer you to equivalent commands that you can use at the command prompt.

Selecting a Single File

In the Shell, you'll want to select one or more file names before attempting to move, copy, delete, or rename the file. When a file is selected, its icon is darkened or (on a text screen) its name is marked with a > symbol. To select a file with a mouse:

- Click the file name.   *Mouse*

Or, with a keyboard,

1. Press Tab or Shift+Tab until the highlighter is in the   *Keyboard*
   Files List.
2. Use Home, End, PgUp, PgDn, ↑, ↓ and/or the first letter of
   a file name to highlight the name of the file you want to
   select.

You can then move to another area, or activate the menus, and the currently selected file name will remain selected.

Selecting Multiple Files

You can also select groups of files, whether they are adjacent in the Files area or not.

Selecting Adjacent File Names

To select a group of file names that are listed consecutively in the Files List,

Mouse

1. Click the name of the first file in the group you want to select.

2. Hold down the Shift key, then click the last file name in the group you want to select.

Or...

Keyboard

1. Move the highlighter to the first file name in the group you want to select.

2. Hold down the Shift key while pressing the ↓ or ↑ key to scroll through other file names.

If you want to select multiple groups of file names,

Mouse

1. Select your first group of file names, as described in the previous section.

2. Hold down the Ctrl key while clicking the first file name in the next group.

3. Hold down Ctrl+Shift while clicking the last item of the next group.

Or...

Keyboard

1. Press Shift+F8 *before* selecting the first group of file names (the word *ADD* appears in the Action bar near the bottom of the screen).

2. Move to the first file name in the group you want to select, and press the space bar.

3. Hold down the Shift key, and highlight any group of file names with the ↓ and/or ↑ keys.

4. Release the Shift key.

5. Repeat steps 2, 3, and 4 above until all the groups are selected.

6. Press Shift+F8 after selecting all the groups.

Selecting Non-Adjacent File Names

To select groups of file names that are not listed consecutively in the Files area,

Mouse

- Hold down the Ctrl key as you click each file name that you want included in the list.

Or...

Keyboard

1. Press Shift+F8 (the word ADD appears in the Action bar near the bottom of the screen).

2. Use the ↑, ↓, and other movement keys to move the highlighter to any other file name you want to select.

3. Press the space bar to select the currently highlighted file name.

4. Press Shift+F8 again to remove the ADD indicator.

To select a group of files with similar dates or extensions, first choose Options ⇒ File Display Options and change the sort order to Date or Extension. When you return to the Files List, all the files with identical dates or extensions will be in adjacent groups.

Selecting from Multiple Directories

If you want to select files from multiple directories,

1. Choose Options ⇒ Select Across Directories.

2. Select files from any directory as described above, then switch to any other directory, and select files from that

directory. You can select files from as many directories as you wish.

See "Searching for Files" below and "Dual Files List" in Step 10 for additional ways to select files from multiple directories.

Selecting All Files

To select all the files currently displayed in the Files List:

- Choose Files ⟹ Select All, or press Ctrl+/.

You can choose Options ⟹ File Display Options to display a particular file-name pattern, such as *.BAT, then choose Files ⟹ Select All to quickly select all those files.

Deselecting Files

To deselect ("unselect") a selected file,

Mouse

- Hold down the Ctrl key and click the name of the file you want to deselect.

Or...

Keyboard

1. If ADD does not appear in the Action bar, press Shift+F8.
2. Use the ↑ and ↓ keys to move the highlighter to any selected file name.
3. Press the space bar to deselect the file name.

If you want to deselect all the currently selected file names,

- Select File ⟹ Deselect All (or press Ctrl+\).

Controlling Confirmation Boxes

As a safety net, the Shell offers confirmation boxes when you delete, move, or copy files. Three types of confirmation are available:

- **Confirm on Delete**: Asks for permission before deleting files.

- **Confirm on Replace**: Displays the name, size, and date of any file that's about to be replaced, and the file that's about to replace it, then asks for permission to replace.

- **Confirm on Mouse Operation**: Asks for permission before completing copy/move operations performed with a mouse.

The confirmation boxes (generally) provide these options:

- **Yes**: Proceed with the replacement/deletion.

- **No**: Do not replace/delete this file, but proceed with other selected files (if any).

- **Cancel**: Do not delete/replace this file, and do not continue with other selected files.

Confirmation boxes appear only if activated. Here's how to activate or deactivate confirmation boxes:

Turning confirmation on/off

1. Select Options ⇒ Confirmation.
2. Click or press the space bar to activate (put an X in) or deactivate (clear) any confirmation options.
3. Press ↵ or select OK.

Searching For Files

If you can't remember which directory you've stored a particular file on, or you want access to a certain type of file across directories (such as all .BAK files), follow these steps:

1. Select the drive you want to search from the Drives area of the Shell.

2. Select File ⇒ Search.

3. Enter the name of the file you want to search for, or a file name template (such as *.BAK or MAR??.DOC).

4. To search all directories, make sure the Search Entire Disk checkbox is checked (or clear it if you want to search the current directory only).

5. Press ↵ or select OK.

A list of files, including the path, appears on the screen. You can select individual files, or groups of files from this screen just as you can within the Files List of the Shell. The menu bar appears at the top of the screen, so that you can perform basic file operations, such as moving, copying, and deleting (covered in Step 9) from this screen.

To return to the normal Shell screen,

•   Press Esc, or select View ⇒ Program/File Lists.

Copying Files

Once you've selected a file name, or group of file names, you can copy those files. To do so:

1. Select File ⇒ Copy (or press F8).

2. In the *To:* portion of the dialog box, enter the complete path to copy the files to.

3. Press ↵ or select OK.

Note that the path you enter must be an existing directory, and must use proper DOS syntax. For example, enter **A:** for the root directory of the disk in drive A, or **C:\WP51\OLDSTUFF** for the OLDSTUFF subdirectory under the WP51 directory.

If any files will be replaced during the operation, and you've activated Confirm on Replace, DOS will ask for permission before it replaces any files.

Copying to the Same Directory

You can copy a file to a different name on the same directory. For example, you can make a copy of MYLETTER.WP named MYCOPY.WP. To do so,

1. Select the file you want to copy (you can select only one file name in this operation).

2. Select File ⇒ Copy (or press F8).

3. Type the name of the copied file.

4. Press ↵ or select OK.

Copying by Dragging

With a mouse, you can quickly copy one or more files to any directory by dragging the file names to a directory or drive icon. Here's how:

1. Select the file or files you want to copy.

2. Hold down the Ctrl key, hold down the active mouse button, and then drag the icon to the directory or drive to which you want to copy the files.

3. Release the mouse button, then release the Ctrl key.

If Confirm on Mouse Operation is on, you'll be asked for permission to complete the copy. If you drag the file icon to a disk drive icon, the files will be copied to the root directory of that drive.

While you're dragging an icon to a different area of the Shell, the icon turns into an international "No" symbol when you're in an area to which the icon cannot be copied.

Copying Files at the Command Prompt

If you want to copy files at the command prompt without going into the Shell, use the Copy command with this general syntax:

```
copy from to
```

For example, entering the command

```
copy *.* a:\
```

copies all the files *from* the current drive and directory *to* the root directory of the disk in drive A.

If you omit the second parameter, the current drive and directory are assumed. For example, the command

```
copy a:\*.*
```

contains only one parameter, a:*.*. Thus, it copies all the files *from* the root directory of the disk in drive A to the current drive and directory. For more information and examples, enter **help copy** at the command prompt to view the online documentation.

Moving Files

After selecting a file (or files) from the Files area, you can follow these steps to move the selected file(s):

1. Select File ⇒ Move (or press F7).

2. In the *To:* portion of the dialog box that appears, enter the complete path of the directory to which you want to move the files (e.g. **A:** or **C:\WP\EXTRA**).

3. Press ↵ or select OK.

Moving by Dragging

With a mouse, you can move one or more files from one directory to another drive or directory by dragging.

1. Select the file or files you want to move.

2. Hold down the Alt key, then hold down the mouse button.

3. Drag the icon to the drive icon or directory name to which you want to move the files.

4. Release the mouse button, then release the Alt key.

As with copying, if the Confirm on Mouse Operation confirmation is on, you'll be asked for permission to complete the move. If you drag the file icon to a disk-drive icon, the files will be moved to the root directory of that drive.

See Step 9 for tips on using the Dual File List to move and copy files by dragging them from one drive\ directory to another.

Moving Files at the Command Prompt

DOS 6 is the first version of DOS to contain a MOVE command. It requires this general syntax:

```
move from to
```

For example, the command

```
move c:\newfiles\*.* c:\oldfiles
```

moves all the files from the c:\newfiles directory to the c:\oldfiles directory. For more information and examples, enter **help move** to get the online documentation for that command.

Renaming Files

To change the name of a selected file (or group of files),

1. Select File ⇒ Rename.

2. Fill in the *New Name:* portion of the dialog box with the new name of the file.

You cannot enter a different drive or directory name to move the file elsewhere (use the Move options described earlier instead). If several files were selected when you chose Rename, you'll be prompted to enter a new name for each selected file.

Renaming Files at the Command Prompt

At the command prompt, you can use the RENAME command (or its abbreviated form REN) to rename a file. Use the following general syntax:

```
ren oldname newname
```

For example, the command

```
ren myfave.txt myfave.old
```

changes the name of the file MYFAVE.TXT to MYFAVE.OLD. For more information, see RENAME in the online documentation.

Deleting Files

After you've selected a file name (or group of files), you can follow these steps to delete them from your disk:

- Select File ⇒ Delete (or press Del).

If Confirm on Delete is active, you'll be asked for permission before DOS deletes the files. Select OK to delete the file.

Deleting Files at the Command Prompt

You can also delete files if you're at the command prompt. Be forewarned, however, that DOS doesn't let you change your mind if you start from the command prompt, *unless* you use the /P switch.

To delete files, you can use either of the following commands (don't type the brackets if you use the optional switch):

```
del filename [/p]
```

or

```
erase filename [/p]
```

It doesn't matter which you use—they're just two different versions of the same command. For more information and examples, see DEL or ERASE in the online documentation.

If you accidentally delete a file, or group of files, you may be able to recover them. See Step 9 for more information.

Viewing the Contents of a File

In the Shell, you can follow these steps to view the contents of a file:

1. Select any single file name in the Files List area (only one file name can be selected).

2. Choose File ⇒ View File Contents (or press F9).

If the file contains only text (such as a .BAT or .TXT file), you'll be able to see the text clearly. If the file contains instructions for the computer (as a .COM or .EXE file would), those characters will appear as gibberish. After viewing the file contents, you can press Esc to return to the Shell.

Viewing File Contents at the Command Prompt

To view the contents of a file at the command prompt, use the general syntax

```
type filename
```

For example, you could enter the command

```
type c:\autoexec.bat
```

to view the contents of your AUTOEXEC.BAT file. If the file is large and you want to scroll a page at a time, you can use the syntax

```
type filename | more
```

For more information and examples, see the online documentation for the TYPE command.

Hiding and Protecting Files

A file can be assigned any of the following attributes:

- **Hidden**: File name does not appear on the screen (unless you've selected Options ⇒ File Display Options and activated Display Hidden/System Files).

- **System**: Identifies an MS-DOS system file.

- **Archive**: File has been modified since the last backup operation (backing up assigns archive status automatically).

- **Read-Only**: File contents can be viewed but not modified; extra warning on delete.

After you select a file (or several files), you can change the attributes.

1. Select File ⇒ Change Attributes.

2. If several files are selected, you can change their attributes one at a time (by pressing ↵), or change attributes for all the files at once (press ↓ then ↵, or click 2).

3. To assign/deassign an attribute, click the attribute, or position the highlighter with ↑ and ↓, then press the space bar.

4. When done, select OK.

If you opted to assign attributes to files one at a time, you'll be prompted to assign attributes for each selected file.

**Checking and Changing
Attributes at the Command Prompt**

At the command prompt, you can use the ATTRIB command to check/change file attributes. See ATTRIB in the online documentation for more information and examples.

Floppy disks come in two basic sizes, 5.25" and 3.5". The 5.25" disks are available in several capacities, the most common being 360K and 1.2MB. The 3.5" disks are available in 720K and 1.4MB capacities. One *byte* equals one character, a *kilobyte* (K) is about a thousand bytes, and a *megabyte* (MB) is about a million bytes. The correct disk size and capacity for your particular computer are determined by the floppy drives installed.

About Formatting

New blank disks may or may not be *formatted* for use on your computer when you buy them. Unformatted disks must be formatted before you can use them.

Never format any disk that already has information on it, such as a program you've just purchased. Formatting a disk will completely erase any information stored on it.

Determining Whether a Disk is Formatted

To find out whether a disk is formatted, you should first check for information on the disk:

Avoiding formatting mistakes

1. Insert the floppy disk in question in drive A (or B).

2. Select that drive from the Drives area in the Shell. Or, if you're at the command prompt, check the floppy's directory (enter **dir a:** or **dir b:**).

If the disk *isn't* formatted, you'll see a "General failure..." message indicating that DOS cannot read the disk. That's good, because it means it's safe to format the disk. (In the Shell, press Esc and then reselect drive C. At the prompt, type A to choose Abort.)

If DOS *can* read the disk, that disk is already formatted. Therefore, you shouldn't reformat it unless you're willing to lose all the information that's on the disk.

The most disastrous mistake you can make on a computer is to reformat the hard disk. (I tell you this because people make this mistake quite often!) Basically, you *never* want to format a hard disk unless you're *absolutely* certain you can live without *any* of the information on that disk (in other words, don't reformat the hard disk unless you've backed up all the files you need; see Step 8). Whenever you're formatting a disk, pay close attention to the messages that appear on the screen, and respond accordingly, to make sure you're *not* about to reformat a hard (nonremovable) disk by accident.

Formatting a Floppy Disk from the Shell

To format a floppy disk, starting from the Shell:

1. Insert the unformatted disk in drive A or B.

2. Select Disk Utilities from the Main Program List near the bottom of the screen.

3. Select Format.

4. If you are formatting the disk in drive B, type **b:**; otherwise leave the default **a:** in the text box.

5. Select OK or press ↵.

6. When you see the *Insert new diskette...* message, press ↵ to continue.

7. When formatting is complete, you'll see the message *Volume label (11 characters, ENTER for none)?*.

You can add an electronic volume label up to 11 characters in length, which will appear on the screen when you look at the contents of the disk in the future. Press ↵ after typing the label. If you choose not to add a volume label, just press ↵ without typing any characters first.

The screen then displays the total disk space available and other information about the disk, followed by the prompt *Format another (Y/N)?*. If you want to format another disk, type **Y** to answer Yes and follow the instructions on the screen. Otherwise, type **N** and press ↵.

Formatting from the Command Prompt

If you're at the command prompt and want to format a floppy disk, insert the unformatted disk in drive A or B. Then, enter the FORMAT command followed by the drive that contains the disk you want to format. For example, to format the floppy in drive A, you'd enter the command

```
format a:
```

Or, to format the floppy in drive B, you'd enter

```
format b:
```

Follow the instructions and answer the prompts that appear on the screen.

What's the Difference Between Format and Quick Format?

If you use the Shell to format a disk, you may notice two formatting options, Quick Format and Format. You can use Quick Format to reformat a previously formatted disk; that's basically the same as erasing the disk. Use the Format option when you're formatting a new disk.

Formatting for Lower Density Drives

If you have high-capacity (1.4MB or 1.2MB) drives, you can format the disks in those drives for use in lower-capacity drives. This is handy when, for instance, you need to copy files to a disk for use in a computer without high-capacity drives.

Floppy disk compatibility

Invalid
media...

If you try to format a low-density disk in a high-density drive, you'll most likely just get an "Invalid media..." message. Formatting the disk at the lower density will often correct this problem.

Never try to format a low-density disk as a high-density disk. To format a 360K disk in a 1.2MB drive, add a blank space and the switch /f:360 to the right of the a: or b: in the dialog box or command. For example, if you're using the Shell you'd enter this in the dialog box:

```
a: /f:360
```

If you're using the command prompt, you'd enter this command:

```
format a: /f:360
```

To format a 720K 3.5" floppy in a high-density drive, use /f:720 instead of /f:360.

Formatting Bootable Disks

System
tracks

Whenever you turn on your computer, one of the first things it does is search the disk in drive A for the operating system's *system tracks*, which provide information the computer needs to get started. (You can see the drive light come on as it does this.) If drive A is empty, the computer automatically searches the hard disk for the system tracks. Once it finds them, the computer starts (or "boots up").

A disk that has a copy of the system tracks is called a *bootable disk*, because the computer can "boot itself up" from that disk. Normally when you format a floppy disk, it *doesn't* receive a copy of the system tracks. When you try to boot a computer from a non-bootable disk, you just get the error message *Non-system disk or disk error* until you put in a bootable disk and press any key.

It's good to keep a bootable floppy disk around, stored in a safe place. That way, if some unpleasant disaster makes it impossible for you to boot from your hard disk, you can boot from the floppy instead.

You can format a floppy disk, and copy the system tracks to it at the same time, by using the optional /s switch. For example, if you're using the Shell and formatting a floppy in drive A, you'd fill in the dialog box (in the fourth step) like this:

/s

If you're at the command prompt, just put the /s switch at the end of the command (preceded by a space of course), like this:

format a: /s

Copying the System Tracks Only

If you're using preformatted disks, or simply want to convert a standard floppy to a bootable floppy, you can easily copy just the system tracks from your hard disk to the floppy. Use the SYS command followed by the name of the drive you're copying the system tracks from and the drive you're copying them to. For example, to copy the system tracks from drive C to the floppy in drive A, you'd enter this command at the command prompt:

sys c: a:

For more information on formatting and the SYS command, look up FORMAT and SYS in your online DOS documentation.

"Unformatting" a Disk

If you do ever accidentally reformat a disk (hard or floppy), all may not be lost. See Step 9 for recovery procedures.

Copying Diskettes

To make an exact copy of a diskette, for use as a backup copy in case your original gets destroyed, follow these steps:

Copying entire diskettes

1.   Place the disk you want to copy in drive A.

2. If you have two identical floppy drives, place a blank diskette (it need not be formatted) in drive B. Do so only if the drives are identical; for example, both 5.25" 1.2MB, or both 3.5" 720K.

3. If you have not done so already, select Disk Utilities from the Main Program List near the bottom of the screen.

4. Select Disk Copy (by double-clicking or highlighting and pressing ↵).

5. If you have two identical drives, press ↵ or select OK to accept the suggested **a: b:**. Otherwise, change the **a: b:** to **a: a:** and press ↵ (or select OK).

6. Follow the instructions that appear on the screen. Keep in mind that the *source* disk is the original disk that you are copying, and the *target* disk is the one that's receiving the copied files.

Copying individual files

At the command prompt, you can use the DISKCOPY command to perform the same job. But remember, to copy individual files, or copy from one type of disk to another, you must use the COPY command, the XCOPY command, or the Shell techniques described in Step 6. DISKCOPY is *only* for making an exact duplicate of an entire disk. Look up DISKCOPY in the online documentation for more information.

Creating a Directory

Typically, when you install a large program on your hard disk, that program automatically creates a directory for itself and any auxiliary files. However, to organize groups of files so that you can work with them more easily, you'll often want to create directories on to your own, either on a hard disk or floppies. You can use either the Shell, or the command prompt, to create a directory.

Directory names

Directory names, like file names, can be up to eight characters in length (no blank spaces), and be followed by a period and extension up to three characters in length. It's customary, however, to omit the extension in directory names to avoid confusing them with file names.

The Shell offers the easiest and most visual way to create a directory:

1. Select the drive on which you want to create a directory.

2. In the Directory Tree area, click a directory that's one level higher than the level you want. For example, to create a first-level directory (the most common case), click the root directory (\) at the top of the tree. To create a subdirectory beneath an existing directory (for example, C:\WPWIN\DOCS), click the name of the directory that will be above this new directory (C:\WPWIN in this example).

3. Select File ⇒ Create Directory from the menus.

4. Type the new directory name, then press ↵ or select OK.

The new directory name appears in the tree, in alphabetical order according to its level in the tree. To select the new directory, click its name (it will be empty, since you just created it).

Creating a Directory at the Command Prompt

To create a directory starting at the command prompt, you can use the MKDIR command, or its abbreviated form, MD. If you want the directory to be one level below the root, precede the name with a backslash. For example, to create a directory named TEMP that's one level below the root, you'd enter the command:

```
md \temp
```

See the MKDIR command entry in the online documentation if you want more information and examples.

Renaming a Directory

If you're in the Shell, you can change the name of a directory:

1. In the Directory Tree area, highlight the name of the directory that you want to change.

2. Choose File ⇒ Rename.

3. Type the new name, then press ↵ or select OK.

Renaming a Directory at the Command Prompt

At the command prompt, you can use the MOVE command (not RENAME) to rename a directory. Use this basic syntax:

```
move oldname newname
```

For example, this command would change the directory named LORNA to LAURA:

```
move lorna laura
```

Permission denied

Now this is going to sound strange, but you can only use the MOVE command or the Shell to *rename* the directory. You cannot move the directory to some new position in the hierarchy. For instance, if you try to move a directory named TEMP so that it's below a directory named PROJECTS using a command like **move temp projects\temp** DOS will say *Unable to open source* and refuse your request. Go figure.

Deleting a Directory

You can remove any existing directory from the tree *only if it does not contain any files, and only if there are no subdirectories beneath it.*

To remove an empty directory while you're in the Shell:

1. In the Directory Tree area, highlight the name of the directory that you want to delete.
2. Press Delete (Del) or choose File ⇒ Delete.
3. Select Yes if you're sure you want to delete that directory.

Emptying a directory

If you receive a message that begins "Deletion Error...," then the directory is not empty. Select Close, then erase or move any files on that directory (see Step 6), and/or remove any subdirectories beneath that directory.

Removing a Directory at the Command Prompt

If you're at the command prompt, you can use the RMDIR command or its abbreviated form, RD, to remove an empty directory. Also, you must not be in the directory that you want to remove. For example, suppose you've just erased all the files from a directory named LORNA (using **erase *.***); now you want to remove the LORNA directory itself. First, you could move up the tree by one level (using the shortcut command **cd**), then use the RD command to delete the directory, as in the commands below:

```
cd \
rd \lorna
```

As in the Shell, your request will be denied if the directory is not empty, or there are directories beneath the one you're trying to delete.

Don't Remove . or ..

When you use the DIR command, you may see these two directory names listed above the file names:

```
.   <DIR>
..  <DIR>
```

Oddly, these are not files at all. Rather, the dot (.) is an abbreviation for the current directory, and the double-dot (..) is an abbreviation for the parent directory—the directory that's one level above the current one.

You can't remove those directories—they're always there. In fact you especially *don't* want to try to erase them by entering a command like **erase .** (which will erase all the files on the current directory), or **erase ..** (which will erase all the files on the parent directory!). If you do accidentally erase files, and discover the mistake right away, you can probably recover the deleted files using UNDELETE, as discussed in Step 9.

The New DELTREE Command

DOS 6 offers another way to delete a directory—the DELTREE command. DELTREE is quick because it doesn't require that you empty the directory of files and subdirectories. Instead, it just gives you a brief moment to change your mind.

For example, suppose you want to delete a directory named \OLDSTUFF and its subdirectory named \OLDSTUFF\TEMP on drive C. You could first enter the command **cd ** to switch to the root directory. Then, enter the command **deltree c:\oldstuff** at the command prompt. You'd see a message like:

```
Delete directory "c:\oldstuff" and all its
subdirectories? [yn]
```

Here, you have to think very carefully before you act. If you choose Yes, you'll lose all the files on the \OLDSTUFF directory, and all the files on the \OLDSTUFF\TEMP directory as well. You'll also lose the directories themselves, which makes it nearly impossible to change your mind and undelete the files.

So don't use DELTREE unless you're *absolutely* sure you know what you're deleting, and don't be too quick to respond with a Y when prompted for permission. For more information, you can enter **help deltree** at the command prompt.

Moving a Directory

Suppose you want to move a directory to a different level in the Directory Tree hierarchy—for example, you want to move a directory named ARTICLE so that it's beneath a directory named PROJECTS.

The easiest way to make this kind of move is in the Windows File Manager. There, you can just drag the directory name from its current level to whatever new level you want.

If you don't have Windows, you can use DOS to get the job done in a roundabout way. Using the general Shell techniques described earlier, you would first need to create a new directory at the new location. Then move (don't copy) all the files from the original directory location to the new directory. After you're sure all the files have been moved successfully to the new location, you can delete the directory name in the old location.

Getting Disk, Directory, and File Information

In the Shell, you can get information about any file, directory, or disk drive by following these steps:

1. Select any single file name (if you are interested in a particular file).

2. Select Options ⟹ Show Information.

The dialog box displays the file information shown in Figure 7.1. This information includes:

*   Name of the currently selected or highlighted file, or the first file in a selected group

*   Attributes assigned to the currently selected file (r = read-only, h=hidden, s=system, a=archive)

*   Drives that contain the selected files

*   Number of currently selected files per drive

*   Total bytes used by all selected files (useful for learning how much disk space you'll need to copy or move selected files)

*   Name of currently selected directory

*   Bytes stored on the current directory

*   Number of files on current directory

*   Volume label of disk (if any)

*   Total disk capacity

- Number of bytes available on disk
- Total number of files stored on the disk
- Total number of directories on the disk

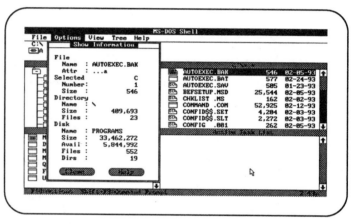

Figure 7.1: The Show Information display for a file named C:\AUTOEXEC.BAK

After viewing the Show Information window, click Close to return to the Shell.

Getting Information at the Command Prompt

You can use the CHKDSK (check disk) command at the prompt to get some information about a disk. This information is similar to the "Disk" information displayed by Show Information in the Shell and also includes the total memory available and free (in bytes). For example, to get information about the disk in drive A, enter the command:

```
chkdsk a:
```

Other commands that provide useful information include DIR and MEM, which you can look up in the online documentation. Also, the MSD (Microsoft diagnostics) program that comes with DOS 6 provides lots of detailed information about your system.

Backing Up a Hard Disk

Because there is always the outside chance that a hard disk will crash (which destroys all your files), it's a good idea to back up your hard disk files to floppy disks, removable disks, or network drives. Backups also are useful if you need to transfer many files from one computer to another. Later, you can restore the files if necessary.

You can use the MSBACKUP command to make backups or restore files from backups. Initially, you should back up the entire hard disk. The Backup screen will show how many floppies or how much disk space you'll need to store backups for the files you select and will estimate the amount of time needed to back up the files.

Your initial backup probably will require many floppy disks. You can perform all but the final step of the backup procedure to find out how many you'll need.

Choosing a Backup Type

You can choose any of three backup types to specify which files are backed up:

Backup types

- **Full** backs up every file you select (default setting). Use Full for initial backups and whenever you want to back up all selected files, whether they were changed or not.

- **Incremental** backs up files that have changed since your last full or incremental backup and switches the archive flag to prevent the same files from being backed up in the next incremental backup unless they change again. Use Incremental if you want to keep interim copies of all your data files as they change.

- **Differential** backs up files that have changed since your last full backup, leaving the archive status unchanged so that you can back up the same files again during the next differential backup. Use Differential if you want a single backup set that contains all files changed since the last full backup.

Understanding Setup Files

Setup files store backup preferences

Your selections about which files will be backed up and how the backups will be performed are stored in *setup files* with an extension of .SET (the default setup file name is DEFAULT.SET). You can define different setup files for each type of backup you wish to perform. For example, you might define FULLBACK.SET for full backups, DAILY.SET for differential daily backups, and WEEKLY.SET for incremental weekly backups.

Understanding Backup Sets and Backup Catalogs

Backup sets store data

During the backup process, MSBACKUP creates backup sets and backup catalogs. *Backup sets* contain the actual data backed up and are stored on the backup disk or disks.

Backup catalogs describe backup sets

The *backup catalog* lists relevant information about the files that are backed up. It is stored on the last floppy disk of each backup set and in the \DOS directory of drive C (or wherever the MSBACKUP program files are located). If you need to restore files, you must load the appropriate backup catalog first.

Backup catalog file names uniquely identify each backup set. For example, the name CD31109A.INC has the following meaning:

- **C** is the first drive backed up in the set (drive C).

- **D** is the last drive backed up in the set (drive D).

- **3** is the last digit of the year, as determined by the system date (3 for 1993).

- **11** is the month the backup set was created (11 for November).

- **09** is the day the backup set was created (9).

- A is the sequence letter (from A to Z) of this backup. This letter is incremented each time you make another backup of the same disks on the same day.

- INC reflects the type of backup made: INC (incremental), FUL (full), or DIF (differential).

Using MSBACKUP for DOS

To start MSBACKUP, type **msbackup** and press ↵ at the command prompt. If you haven't performed a disk compatibility test yet, an Alert message may appear. Press ↵ to begin the test, then follow the on-screen prompts. You'll need two floppy disks of the same type to complete the test, and all data on these disks will be overwritten.

Starting MSBACKUP

The options available on the main Microsoft Backup screen are: Backup (to back up files), Restore (to restore files), Compare (to compare backup disks with original files), Configure (to modify screen appearance and choose backup devices), and Quit (to exit MSBACKUP). The File menu allows you to open, save, delete, and print setup files and exit MSBACKUP. The Help menu provides help with backup procedures.

Main Backup screen options

Moving Around Screens and Selecting Options

You can use the following keyboard techniques to move around screens and select options. If you prefer, you can click with your mouse instead.

Techniques for using MSBACKUP

- To select a button or open a menu, press Alt plus the highlighted letter in the name (for example, Alt+B selects the Backup button and Alt+F opens the File menu). After opening a menu, select an option by typing its highlighted letter.

- To move from button to button or to various areas on the screen, press Tab or Shift+Tab. To select a highlighted button, press ↵.

- To move the selection highlight up or down within a list of options, press ↑ or ↓.

- To check or uncheck a selected item in a list, press the space bar. The space bar toggles your selection on or off.

- To select a radio button option, type the option's high-lighted letter.

To get help, highlight an option and look at the status line at the bottom of the screen. For detailed help, press F1.

To exit MSBACKUP, select File ⇒ Exit from the menus, or select the Quit button from the main Microsoft Backup screen.

Backing Up Files

To back up files,

1. Start MSBACKUP, then select the Backup button. If you've already defined and saved your default Setup file, you can skip to Step 7.

2. To load a different setup file, select Setup File, highlight or click on the file you want, and press ↵ or select Open.

3. To back up a different drive, or an additional drive, select Backup From. Highlight the drive you want and press the space bar, or click on the drive.

4. To choose a different drive, select Backup To, type or click on the highlighted letter or number of the drive you want, and press ↵ or select OK.

5. To select the files to be backed up, choose Select Files. Highlight the drive, directory, or file you're interested in. Press the space bar or click the mouse to select (check) or deselect (uncheck) it in the backup list; repeat this until you've selected all the files you want to back up. Press ↵ or select OK when you're finished.

6. To select a different backup type, select Backup Type, then select Full, Incremental, or Differential, and press ↵ or select OK. Full, the default option, backs up *all* selected files.

7. To start the backup, select Start Backup and follow the instructions that appear on the screen.

As you remove each backup disk, be sure to label it with the name of the backup catalog file and disk number within the backup set, so that you'll know which disks to use when restoring files later. Use the DIR command, if necessary, to determine the catalog file name.

To save your backup set at any time, choose File ⇒ Save Setup or File ⇒ Save Setup As from the menus.

Backing Up Altered Files Only

After the initial backup, you can save a lot of time by backing up only files that are new or were modified since the last backup. To perform the partial backup, follow the first five steps above. In step 6, select either Incremental or Differential, then complete step 7.

Restoring Backup Files

If your hard disk crashes and needs to be replaced or reformatted, or you need to transfer files to another computer or hard disk, you can restore your files from backups.

To restore files,

1. Start MSBACKUP, then select the Restore button. If you want all the default selections, skip to step 5.

2. To choose a different backup catalog, select Backup Set Catalog, highlight the catalog you want, press the space bar or click the mouse, and then press ↵ or select Load.

    If you've lost or deleted the hard disk copy of the backup catalog, you can select Catalog and rebuild the catalog.

3. To restore from a different drive, select Restore From, select the drive you want, and press ↵ or select OK.

4. To restore the files to a location other than their original location, select Restore To, select the option you want, and press ↵ or select OK.

5. To select files to be restored, choose Select Files and check the files you want. Press ↵ or select OK when you're finished.

6. To restore the selected files, select Start Restore and follow the screen prompts.

Step 9

Recovering from Mishaps

15

To paraphrase a contemporary saying, stuff happens. In this step we'll look at ways to recover from two of the most troublesome (and common) mistakes people make when using computers: deleting files accidentally, and accidentally reformatting a disk that already contains files.

An Ounce of Prevention...

Before we get into the wonders of undeleting and unformatting, it's important to keep in mind that these techniques are not foolproof. The reason it's possible to undelete files at all is that DOS doesn't actually erase the contents of a file you delete; it simply stops keeping track of where it put that file. If you create, save, or copy other files after a deletion, DOS may overwrite the space occupied by the deleted file, and you may not be able to recover that file. So it's important to keep two points in mind:

- A backup copy of important files is always your best defense.

- If you do accidentally delete files or reformat a disk, you should perform the recovery right away. The recovery techniques presented in this step assume that you've done nothing else since the deletion.

Delete Protection

DOS 6 offers an important form of "preventive medicine"; you can specify any of three levels of *delete protection*:

- **Delete Sentry**: Offering the highest level of protection, this option creates a hidden directory named SENTRY, to which deleted files are moved without changing their locations in the file allocation table. The Sentry program uses some memory and disk space.

- **Delete Tracker**: Offering intermediate protection, this method creates a small hidden file named PCTRACKR.DEL, where DOS records the location of a deleted file. When you delete a file, DOS changes the file allocation table so that the deleted file's former location is available for a new file. You can recover the file only if another file has not been placed in its former location. Delete Tracker uses some memory and a little less disk space than the Sentry method.

- **MS-DOS**: Offering the least protection, this is the default method. It doesn't use any memory or disk space, but is the least likely to succeed in recovering a deleted file.

Deciding which deletion protection method is best for you is a trade-off between using up a little memory and disk space for ultimate protection, or using no memory and disk space for minimal protection. Obviously, the less experience you (or other people who use your computer) have with managing files, the more protection you want.

Using Delete Protection

You implement Sentry or Tracker protection by adding switches to the UNDELETE command. It doesn't do any good to change from one level of protection to another *after* you've deleted a file. So you should activate your protection level right after you start your computer. Or, preferably, by adding the appropriate UNDELETE command to your AUTOEXEC.BAT file (Step 17). Your options are:

- **undelete /s** activates the sentry method
- **undelete /t** activates the tracking method

If you don't enter either of those commands, the MS-DOS method is used. Regardless of which level of protection you decide upon, the technique you follow to undelete a file is the same, as discussed in a moment.

Make Sure You're Not the One Who's Lost

Contrary to popular opinion, files don't just disappear. If you can't find
a file, but don't recall specifically deleting that file, chances are you're
just looking in the wrong place. If you know the name of the file and
the drive it's on, you can search across all directories for the file using
either of these techniques. To do so in the Shell:

1. Choose the drive that the file is on, then choose View ⇒
   All Files.

2. To make sure you're getting the complete picture in alphabetical order, choose Options ⇒ File Display Options.
   Make sure the text box next to *Name:* contains *.* and, if
   you want file names listed in alphabetical order, choose
   Name under Sort By. Then press ⏎ or choose OK.

*Searching
from the
Shell*

The Files List now shows the names of all files on the current disk,
in alphabetical order. You can scroll down to where the "missing
file" should appear in the alphabetical sequence. If the file is still on
the disk, its name will be listed and its directory location will appear
next to *Name:* (under Directory) near the left side of the screen. You
need not undelete the file. If you don't see the file, you'll need to
undelete it.

If you're at the command prompt, you can search all the directories
by starting at the root directory and using the /s switch with the DIR
command. For example, suppose you're looking for a file named
myfave. Entering this command at the command prompt:

*Searching
from the
Command
Prompt*

```
dir \myfave*.* /s
```

would search the entire hard disk (drive C) for that file. The
backslash (\) in front of the file name is important, because it
ensures that the search begins at the root directory. If the file exists,
it will be listed under the name of its directory. You need not
undelete the file in that case. But if the file has been deleted and
doesn't exist anywhere on the current drive, you'll see a *File not
found* message.

Undeleting Deleted Files

If you need to undelete a file, use the CD command to switch to the directory where the file was located. Then type **undelete** and press ⏎. You'll be prompted for confirmation on each file, and UNDELETE will use the highest level of deletion tracking available.

Alternatively, you can specify the drive, directory, and name of the file to undelete. You can even use the /all switch to undelete all the files without being prompted for permission. For example, suppose you accidentally used the command *del *.** or *erase *.** or *del .* to delete all the files on a directory named C:\WPWIN\DOCS. You could then enter the command **undelete c:\wpwin\docs*.* /all** to recover all the files on that directory at once.

Using Undelete for Windows

If you have Windows and opted to install Undelete for Windows when you upgraded to DOS 6, you can undelete files via Windows. Start Windows, open the Microsoft Tools group, then double-click the Undelete icon (the one that shows the paper coming out of the trash can). If you need help using the program, press F1.

Undeleting Directories

Some programs, including the Windows File Manager and the DELTREE command in DOS, let you delete an entire directory without first deleting all the files on that directory. This can make for a hefty mistake.

If you need to undelete an entire directory, you must use the Windows version of the Microsoft DOS 6 Undelete program. That is, get to the Windows Program Manager, open the Microsoft Tools group, and double-click the Undelete icon to get to the Microsoft Undelete dialog box.

Within the Microsoft Undelete dialog box, use the Drive/Dir button to move to a directory that's one level above the directory you deleted. Typically you can do that by choosing the parent directory symbol (..). In the list of file names, look for the name of the deleted directory, but with the first letter replaced by a question mark (?), and the <Dir> symbol listed in the Size column. Then click that name, click the Undelete button, and follow the instructions on the screen.

Once you've recovered the directory, use the Drive/Dir button to switch to that recovered directory. You can then use the Undelete button to undelete the files on that directory.

Unformatting an Accidentally Reformatted Disk

If you reformat a disk accidentally, you'll lose all the files on that disk. Depending on the type of formatting you used, it may be possible to recover the files with the command UNFORMAT.

Formatting (and unformatting) a hard disk is never really necessary, and is dangerous unless you know *exactly* what you're doing. To be safe, format (and unformat) floppy disks only!

Which Disks can be Unformatted?

You can unformat just about any recently reformatted disk provided that (1) You didn't use the optional /u switch in the Format command to do an unconditional format, and (2) You haven't stored new information on the disk since it was reformatted.

How to Unformat

To unformat a disk, start at the command prompt and enter the UNFORMAT command followed by a blank space and the name of the drive that contains the disk you want to unformat. For example, to unformat the floppy disk in drive A, you'd enter the command:

```
unformat a:
```

Press ↵, and follow any instructions that appear on the screen.

For More Information...

The information presented here should help you to recover from just about any formatting or deleting mishap. However, if you want more information on these topics, you can look up UNFORMAT, UNDELETE, and FORMAT in the online documentation.

Step 10

Printing, Pausing, and Filing

15

Normally when you enter a command at the DOS prompt, that command displays its output on the screen. As an alternative, you can *redirect* the output of many commands to the printer or to a file.

Sending Output to the Printer

If you want the information that a command normally presents on the screen to appear on the printer instead, end the command line with **>prn**. The output will go to the printer instead of the screen. You may need to eject the page from the printer to see that output, as described later in this Step. Some sample commands with >prn added are listed below:

Command	What it Does
tree \ >prn	Prints a copy of the current drive's directory tree
tree \ /a >prn	Same as above, but without graphics characters
tree \ /a/f >prn	Same as above, but includes names of files on every directory
msd /s >prn	Prints summary information about the computer using the Microsoft Diagnostics program
mem >prn	Prints information about memory
dir /on >prn	Prints an alphabetized list of files on the current directory

Copying the Screen to the Printer

If you simply want to dump a copy of whatever text is on your screen to the printer, you can just press the Print Screen (or Prt Sc on some keyboards) key. On some keyboards, you may have to hold down the Shift key while you press that Print Screen key.

If you're using a page-fed (laser) printer, you'll need to eject the page (as discussed later in this Step) to see the output.

The Print Screen key works only with text. Any graphics characters, including those on the DOS Shell screen, will most likely come out garbled. To print full graphics screens, you'll need a screen-capture program such as Collage Plus.

If Windows is loaded (even if it's suspended), Print Screen's output will go to the Windows Clipboard rather than the printer. See your Windows manual for more information on the Clipboard.

Slaving the Printer

Ctrl+P

While you're at the command prompt, you can "slave" the printer so it mimics just about everything that appears on the screen. All you have to do is press Ctrl+P (once) then go about your business. Remember, if you're using a page-fed printer, you won't see anything happen until the page is full or you eject the page.

To end printer slaving, press Ctrl+P again.

Printing Files

Usually you print a file from the program that created the file. You can, however, print two types of files directly from DOS:

- ASCII text files created with EDIT or some other text editor. These typically have the extension .BAT, .INI, or .TXT.

- Files that were "printed to disk" from a word processing, spreadsheet, or other program. These files often have the extension .PRN.

The simplest way to print such files is to use the general syntax shown below (at the command prompt):

type *filename* **>prn**

Be sure to include the drive and path with the *filename* if the file isn't on the current directory. For example, to print a copy of your AUTOEXEC.BAT file on the root directory of drive C, you'd enter the command

type c:\AUTOEXEC.BAT >prn

When the command prompt reappears, you may need to eject the page from the printer.

Using the PRINT Command

The PRINT command prints in the background, which means you can do other things with your computer while DOS is printing. You might prefer to use the PRINT command when printing a large file. The general syntax for the PRINT command is:

print *filename*

where *filename* is the name of the file you want to print. As usual, if that file isn't on the current directory, you should include the drive and directory name. For example, to print a copy of the CONFIG.SYS file on the root directory of drive C, you'd enter this command:

print c:\config.sys

The first time you use PRINT during any given DOS session, it will probably ask for the name of the device to print to, by displaying the somewhat baffling message:

Name of list device [PRN]:

You can usually just press ↵ to accept the default device, PRN. To use any other printer, enter the name of the port it's connected to. For example, you can type **LPT1** to specify the printer connected to the first parallel port, or **COM1** for the printer connected on the first serial port.

Printing from the Shell

If you want to print files from the Shell, you need to load the PRINT program into memory first. If you've already started the Shell, you can just switch to the \DOS directory, then double-click PRINT.EXE in the Files List. When prompted for a list device, press ↵, then press ↵ once more to return to the Shell.

Once you've loaded PRINT into memory, you can select a file (or files) to print from the Files List. Then, to start printing, choose File ⇒ Print from the Shell menus.

Incidentally, you load the PRINT command automatically before starting the Shell. Simply add the PRINT command, followed by /d: and the port for your printer, to your AUTOEXEC.BAT file. For example, if your printer is connected to the first parallel port, you'd add this command to AUTOEXEC.BAT:

```
print /d:lpt1
```

In the future, PRINT will be loaded automatically whenever you start your computer. As usual, you can get more information by looking up PRINT in your online documentation. For more information on editing AUTOEXEC.BAT, see Step 17.

Pausing the Screen Display

Ctrl+S

Often, the information on the screen scrolls by too quickly to read. There are two ways to slow down scrolling. The first is to press Ctrl+S (S as in Stop) at the moment you want to stop scrolling. To start scrolling again, press any key. With this method, you must be very quick on the keyboard to start and stop just right.

The other way to slow down scrolling is to follow the command with | **more**. For instance, suppose you want to read a file named README.TXT that came with a program you just installed, and that file is stored on the directory named NEWPROG on drive C. Entering this command:

```
type c:\newprog\readme.txt | more
```

would display the contents of that file one screenful at a time. At the bottom of each screen, you'd see the message -- *More* --. You can press any key (or the space bar) when you're ready to move on to the next page.

You can place | **more** at the end of any command that displays text on the screen. For example, you might use it rather than > **prn** in the sample commands shown back in Table 10.1.

Viewing File Contents from the Shell

A better way to view the contents of a text file on your screen is through the Shell. Start up the Shell, go to the appropriate drive and directory, and select the file you want from the Files List. (It should be a text file such as README.TXT or AUTOEXEC.BAT.) Then choose File ⇒ View File Contents, or press F9.

If the text appears garbled, try choosing Display ⇒ ASCII. (If the text still appears garbled, you're probably not looking at a text file. Press Esc to exit.)

You can use the PgUp and PgDn keys to scroll through the text file, but you can't make changes to the contents of the file (though you can with EDIT, discussed in Step 17). When you're finished viewing the file, just press Esc to return to the Shell.

Ejecting a Page From the Printer

If you want to see a partially printed page in a laser printer (or skip to the next page in a tractor-fed printer), you need to *eject* the page.

To do that, you generally take the printer off line (usually by pressing the On Line button), then press the Form Feed (or FF) button to eject the page. To put the printer back on line, press the On Line button again.

If you're at the DOS command prompt, you can use an alternative method where you don't have to touch the printer. Simply type the command shown below, but press Ctrl+L where you see ^L. Notice that there's a blank space before and after the Ctrl+L keypress:

```
echo ^L >prn
```

Press ↵ after typing the command, and the page should eject from the printer. (This works on virtually all printers *except* PostScript printers.)

Sending Output to a File

You can also send the output from any command that displays text to a file, rather than the screen or printer. Follow the command with a > symbol and the drive, directory, and file name. (If you omit the drive and directory, the current drive and directory are assumed.) For example, the command below displays a wide list of all the file names on the disk in drive A (DIR A: /W), and sends that information to a file named FILELIST.TXT on the C:\DOS directory:

```
dir a: /w >c:\dos\filelist.txt
```

Because the output is being sent to a file, you won't see anything on the screen.

Adding Output to an Existing File

The >*filename* redirection method always creates a new file. If you want to *add* new text to the end of an existing file, use the >> symbol instead. For example, suppose you put a different disk in drive A, and want to add the list of file names on that disk to the end of C:\DOS\FILELIST.TXT. You'd now use >> rather than > like this:

```
dir a: /w >>c:\dos\filelist.txt
```

Opening the File You Created

The file you create using > or >> is a text file, which you can open and edit using DOS's EDIT command (Step 17), or any word processor. Then you can make any changes you want, and print the file using whatever commands your program requires. For example, if your word processor has the capability, you could print that list of file names onto a disk label.

Step 11

Double Your Hard Disk Space

45

In this step, you'll learn how to check the status of hard disks with CHKDSK and squeeze more space from your disks by compressing them with the new DOS 6 DoubleSpace utility.

Checking Disk Status with CHKDSK

DOS uses a file allocation table (or "FAT") to track the locations of all files on the disk. Errors can occur in the FAT when a program is interrupted unexpectedly, especially if the computer is in the middle of writing files to disk during a power failure or restart. You should repair such errors, since they can interfere with the normal operation of some programs and can waste space on your hard disk.

Getting a Status Report

You can use CHKDSK (Check Disk) to display space available on a disk and to report any errors there. For example, to display the status of drive C, type **chkdsk c:** and press ↵.

Before using CHKDSK, exit all programs, including the DOS Shell, Windows, and any memory-resident (TSR) programs. If any TSRs are listed in your CONFIG.SYS or AUTOEXEC.BAT file, you must disable them by opening those files through the DOS Editor (Step 17) and changing relevant lines into comments. You *don't* need to exit SMARTDrive.

Recovering Lost File Allocation Units

To correct file allocation errors and update the file allocation table, add the /F switch to CHKDSK, as in **chkdsk c: /f**. If file allocation

FAT tracks files on disk

errors exist, you'll see a message like this:

```
10 lost allocation units found in 3 chains.
Convert lost chains to files?
```

An *allocation unit* is the smallest amount of disk space that can be allocated to a file. These units can be "lost" when a program creates a temporary file due to unexpected conditions.

If you type **Y** (for Yes) in response to the message, DOS will save lost file allocation units as a series of numbered files in the root directory, using the file name format FILE*nnnn*.CHK. You can then switch to the root directory (type **cd **) and view the files using the TYPE command. For example, the command **type file0000.chk** displays the contents of the first file that CHKDSK saved. You can use the DEL command to erase any of these files, or open the data file's application and resave the file under a different name.

If you respond **N** for No, DOS will fix the disk errors but won't save the lost units.

It's a good idea to check the status of *each* hard disk whenever you start your computer, by adding the command **chkdsk *x*:** (replace *x* with a valid drive letter) to AUTOEXEC.BAT.

Fixing Cross-Linked Files

CHKDSK can also detect *cross-linked files*, where two files or directories are recorded as using the same disk space. However, it cannot fix these errors even if you use the /F switch. To fix a cross-linked file, copy the files or directories listed in the cross link message elsewhere and delete the originals. Note that some information in these files may be lost.

CHKDSK can't fix physical errors such as bad disk sectors either. Bad sectors are rendered harmless when you format the disk, so they pose no danger.

Compressing Files on Your Hard Disk

You can use the new DOS 6 program DoubleSpace to compress files to one-half or even one-third their original size. File compression offers an economical way to increase disk storage without going to the expense of purchasing a higher-capacity hard disk. Once you've run DoubleSpace to compress a disk, files are automatically compressed when you write them to that disk and uncompressed when you open them. You refer to a compressed drive by its drive letter, just as for uncompressed drives.

Once you compress a drive, you cannot uncompress it without reformatting the disk completely. Please refer to your DOS manual for detailed troubleshooting procedures.

How DoubleSpace File Compression Works

In an uncompressed file, DOS stores every byte of data. However, most files have repetitive sequences—such as many zeros in a row—which can be identified by length and location and stored in more compact form. DoubleSpace works by copying each uncompressed file as a compressed file, then storing it in a special portion of the hard disk called the compressed volume file (CVF). It then deletes the uncompressed file.

Compressed volume files

The uncompressed portion of the drive is called the *host*; each host drive can contain one or more compressed volume files.

Cleaning House before Compressing Your Files

Before compressing a drive with DoubleSpace, you should

- Exit any programs you are running.

- Back up and then delete unneeded files; for added safety, you should back up the entire hard disk that you'll be compressing.

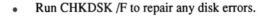

- Run CHKDSK /F to repair any disk errors.

Remember to exit all programs, including the DOS Shell, Windows, and memory resident programs (TSRs) before running DoubleSpace or CHKDSK. Again, you don't need to exit SMARTDrive.

Running DoubleSpace for the First Time

When you're ready to run DoubleSpace for the first time, make sure you've exited all programs, then complete these steps:

1. Type **dblspace** at the command prompt and press ↵.

2. After the introductory screen appears, press ↵ to display the next screen.

3. If you want to compress files on drive C, choose the Express Setup option by pressing ↵. If you want to compress files on a different hard disk drive or create a new (empty) compressed drive, select Custom Setup by pressing ↓ and then pressing ↵.

The first time you run DoubleSpace, DOS runs the DoubleSpace Setup program. The next time you run DoubleSpace, the DoubleSpace Manager program starts. Compressed drives are managed by DBLSPACE.BIN, a portion of DOS that is loaded into memory automatically when you start your computer.

Using DoubleSpace Express Setup

Follow the steps below to complete the Express Setup.

1. After DoubleSpace reports approximately how long the procedure will take, type C to continue. DoubleSpace will show the amount of space available on drive C before and after compressing and will prompt you to restart the computer.

2. Press ↵ to restart the computer.

Now use your computer exactly as you did before compressing the disk. Most of your files will remain on the compressed drive C; however, files that must remain uncompressed for technical reasons will be moved automatically to the uncompressed portion of the hard disk (the *host*). The host drive will be assigned the next unused drive letter, such as drive H.

Using compressed disks

Using DoubleSpace Custom Setup

Custom Setup is useful for compressing an existing drive other than drive C, or for creating a new compressed drive. DoubleSpace will follow a procedure similar to Express Setup.

Managing Compressed Drives with DoubleSpace Manager

After you've compressed the files, you can use the DoubleSpace Manager to check the status of a compressed drive, change the size of compressed drives, create new compressed volumes (even on floppy disks), run CHKDSK, and defragment your disk.

Starting the DoubleSpace Manager

To start the DoubleSpace Manager, exit all programs, then type **dblspace** and press ↵. DoubleSpace will search for existing compressed drives and display the DoubleSpace Manager screen and menus shown in Figure 11.1.

Using the DoubleSpace Manager

You can work with the DoubleSpace Manager as follows.

- To select the drive you want to work with, click its icon in the Drives area, or use the ↑ or ↓ keys to highlight it.

- To get help or find out about other Double Space features, select options from the Help menu or press F1.

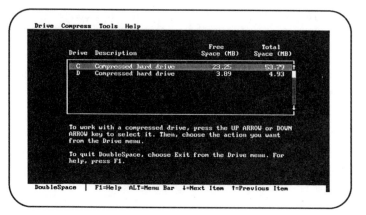

Figure 11.1: The DoubleSpace Manager

- To exit the DoubleSpace Manager, select Drive ⟹ Exit.

Displaying Information about Compressed Drives

To display detailed information about any compressed drive, select the drive in the Drives area of the DoubleSpace Manager, then choose Drive ⟹ Info. Select OK to return to the DoubleSpace Manager screen, or select the Size or Ratio button to adjust the size of the compressed drive or the estimated compression ratio.

You can also display the Compressed Drive Information screen for a drive by double-clicking the compressed drive or highlighting it and pressing ↵.

Changing the Size of Compressed Drives

You can change the size of a compressed drive by adjusting the amount of free space on the *uncompressed* (host) drive. Here are the steps.

1. Select the compressed drive you want to change, then select Drive ⟹ Change Size.

2. When the Change Size screen appears, type in a new amount of free space for the *uncompressed* drive and press ↵.

Compressing Additional Drives

To compress a floppy disk or hard disk that hasn't been compressed yet, follow the steps below.

1. If you're compressing a floppy disk, insert the disk into the floppy drive.

2. Select Compress ⇒ Existing Drive from the main menu. DoubleSpace will scan your computer for compressible drives, which must be formatted and contain at least 0.65MB of free space (1.2MB for the startup hard disk). You cannot compress 360K floppy drives.

3. Select the drive you want to compress and press ↵.

4. Press **C** to begin the process.

Mounting a Floppy Drive

DOS normally treats files on a floppy disk as uncompressed. If files on your floppy disk are compressed, you'll need to inform DOS by "mounting" the floppy drive. Once the drive is mounted, DOS will treat all files on that drive as compressed, even if you put another disk in the drive. If you want to go back to using uncompressed floppy disks in that drive, you'll need to "unmount" the drive.

DoubleSpace will mount the floppy drive automatically if you've just finished compressing it. When you restart (or turn off) your computer, DOS unmounts all floppy drives automatically.

To mount a floppy drive manually, insert the compressed floppy disk into the drive, select Drive ⇒ Mount from the DoubleSpace menus, and follow the screen instructions.

To use an uncompressed disk in a floppy drive that's currently mounted, select Drive ⇒ Unmount and follow the screen instructions. Now you can remove the compressed floppy disk and insert the uncompressed floppy disk in the drive.

Creating New Compressed Drives

You can follow the steps below to create a new compressed drive from free space on an uncompressed hard disk drive. The newly created drive will be compressed, but empty.

1.   Select Compress ⇒ Create New Drive from the DoubleSpace Manager menus.

2.   Highlight the host drive you want to use and press ↵. DoubleSpace will convert that drive's free space to a new compressed drive.

3.   DoubleSpace will display the settings it will use for the new drive. Press ↵ to accept the settings and create the new compressed drive.

Checking the Status of Compressed Drives

To learn the status of a compressed drive's integrity and repair any errors, you can select Tools ⇒ CHKDSK. Then select either the Check button to check the drive without fixing errors, or the Fix button to check the drive and fix any errors that are detected.

Optimizing Speed of Compressed Drives

To reorganize free space (defragment) and optimize performance on a compressed drive, highlight the drive you want to optimize. Then select Tools ⇒ Defragment, and select Yes. (Defragmenting is explained in Step 12.)

Speed Up Your System

You can speed up your system by maximizing your hard disk performance. Two utilities, SMARTDrive and MS-DOS Defragmenter, make this easy. In Step 13, you'll learn yet another way to speed up your system—by using memory efficiently.

You can also speed up operation by creating a memory resident "virtual disk drive." Type **help ramdrive.sys** for more information.

Using SMARTDrive

The SMARTDrive program speeds up your system by using memory, instead of the slower hard disk, whenever possible. It reserves an area (or *cache*) in extended memory where it temporarily stores information read from your hard disk. When an application needs information, SMARTDrive first tries to supply it directly from memory. SMARTDrive also uses memory as a temporary storage place for information that needs to be written to your hard disk. Later, when system resources are in less demand, SMARTDrive stores the information on disk. All this activity takes place safely and automatically, behind the scenes.

*How
SMARTDrive
works*

Do not use SMARTDrive after Windows has started, and do not use it with other disk caching programs.

Activating SMARTDrive

SMARTDrive is added to AUTOEXEC.BAT automatically when you install DOS 6, so you don't have to do anything to ensure that the program starts whenever you start your computer. If you're using DOS 5, you can add the following line to your AUTOEXEC.BAT or CONFIG.SYS file to start SMARTDrive with default settings:

```
c:\dos\smartdrv
```

Using SMARTDrive Double-Buffering

You may need to install SMARTDrive with the *double-buffering* feature if you use EMM386.EXE or run Windows in 386 enhanced mode. Double-buffering is most often necessary if you're using an SCSI hard disk or device, an ESDI device, or an MCA device.

To install SMARTDrive with double-buffering, add the line

```
device=c:\dos\smartdrv.exe /double_buffer
```

to your CONFIG.SYS file (*not* to AUTOEXEC.BAT) and then restart your computer.

When adding SMARTDrive to the CONFIG.SYS file, be sure to list it *after* commands that install HIMEM.SYS and EMM386.SYS. Never use the DEVICEHIGH= command to load SMARTDrive—you might lose data.

Defragmenting Files to Speed up a Hard Disk

Another way to speed up disk access is to rearrange the files on the disk so that they're stored more efficiently. This process is called *defragmenting*.

How Files Become Fragmented

Fragmentation can occur when you frequently load, add to, delete from, and then save files. The more often you add to a file, the more scattered its contents can become on disk. This increases the time required to load and save the file, and it can occur even if your disk has lots of free storage space.

The defragmenting process reorganizes the disk so that, ideally, each file is stored in just one disk area. You can use the MS-DOS Defragmenter program to accomplish this.

Defragmenter can't be used on network drives or on drives created with the command INTERLNK (discussed in Step 15).

Preparing to Defragment a Disk

Before you defragment a disk, you should do all of the following:

- Delete any unnecessary files (Step 6).

- Run the command CHKDSK to make any needed repairs (Step 11).

- For added safety, back up the disk you want to defragment (Step 8).

- Exit all programs.

Never run MS-DOS Defragmenter without first exiting all active programs, including memory-resident programs (TSRs), the DOS Shell, and Windows. You don't need to exit SMARTDrive.

Defragmenting Your Disk Files

To optimize your file storage by running MS-DOS Defragmenter, follow these steps.

1. Type **defrag** and press ↵. The program will ask which disk you want to optimize.

2. Highlight or click on the desired disk and press ↵ or select OK (or simply type the drive letter, such as **C**).

MS-DOS Defragmenter provides lots of on-line help. For assistance, highlight a menu option or go to the dialog box you need help with, and then press F1.

3. MS-DOS Defragmenter will analyze the selected disk. If the drive contains fragmented files, a recommendation screen will appear. You can select Optimize (press ↵) to begin optimizing immediately. Or select Configure (type **C**) if you wish to change the optimization method or sort order

used. If no files are fragmented, simply press ↵ to clear the message that appears.

The Optimize menu shown in Figure 12.1 will appear after optimization is complete and whenever you select Configure from a dialog box.

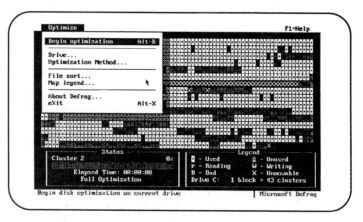

Figure 12.1: The Optimize menu

Note: If you've compressed the selected drive with DoubleSpace (Step 11), the DoubleSpace defragment program will run automatically. You can also defragment compressed disks by selecting Tools ⇒ Defragment from the DoubleSpace Manager menus.

Understanding the Optimize Menu

Optimize menu options

The Optimize menu provides several useful options. The most important are listed below.

- **Begin Optimization:** Defragments the selected disk with the configuration options you have selected.

- **Drive:** Allows you to select the drive you wish to optimize.

- **Optimization Method:** Allows you to select one of two optimization methods (described below).

- **File Sort:** Allows you to sort all files in all directories (described below).

- **Exit:** Returns to the command prompt.

You can also specify options on the DEFRAG command line. Type **help defrag** from the command prompt for more information.

Selecting an Optimization Method

To select an optimization method, choose Optimization ⇒ Optimization Method. Then choose Full Optimization if you want the best performance gain and you're willing to wait a while for the process to complete, or choose Unfragment Files Only if you're in a hurry and you're not worried about squeezing that last iota of performance out of the system.

Full Optimization moves directories to the front of the disk, defragments all files, and moves all gaps to the end of the disk. Unfragment Files Only does not optimize directory placement and leaves unfilled gaps scattered around the disk.

Selecting the File Sort Order

By default, MS-DOS Defragmenter stores files in the same order they had when the process began. To change the sort order for file names in the directory, select Optimize ⇒ File Sort, then select the sort criterion you want. Type or click on **U** to leave files Unsorted, **N** to sort by file Name, **E** to sort by file Extension, **D** to sort by Date & Time last modified, or **S** to sort by Size. Next, press ↓ and select a sort order. Type or click on **A** for Ascending (A to Z) or **D** for Descending (Z to A). Then press ↵ or select OK.

Sorting file directories

Note: File sorting does not affect the physical positioning of the data on the disk.

Thanks for the Memory

DOS (particularly DOS 6) offers tools that help you find out how much memory is available and that optimize your computer's memory use automatically, so that your system can run at peak efficiency.

Understanding Computer Memory

Memory is an essential part of every computer system. All programs must be loaded into memory to run, and data passes through memory on its way to and from the disk. Turning off or restarting your computer deletes information from memory.

Modern computers use five types of memory:

Types of memory

- **Conventional memory** ("standard RAM") is up to 640K on most systems. This area is managed automatically by DOS. All DOS-based applications require conventional memory.

- **Upper memory** (also called *reserved* memory) is the 384K of storage between 640K and 1MB that typically is used to control the monitor, hard disk, and other devices.

- **Extended memory** (also called XMS) is the area above 1MB. Windows, Windows applications, and other programs use this area. A memory manager such as HIMEM.SYS coordinates and manages the use of extended memory on your computer.

- **High memory** is the first 64K of extended memory. Windows and some applications use high memory. You can also load DOS into high memory to free up space for programs that require more conventional memory.

- **Expanded memory** offers another way to provide memory beyond 1MB. Lotus 1-2-3 and other applications that conform to the Lotus/Intel/Microsoft Expanded Memory

Specification (LIM EMS) use expanded memory. It is installed on a memory board and managed with a device driver called an *expanded memory manager.*

Expanded memory can be slower and more cumbersome for programs to use than extended memory. If you have an 80386 or 80486 system with extended memory, you can use the EMM386 utility to run programs that normally require expanded memory. This way, you won't have to install an expanded memory board and driver.

Learning about Your System's Memory Use

You can type **mem** and press ↵ to learn how your system is using memory. MEM can show the total memory in use, how much memory is free (available), and how programs are using memory at the moment.

You can add the following DOS 6 switches to the MEM command line to obtain additional information about memory usage or make MEM more convenient to use.

- **/page** (or **/p**) displays memory information one screen at a time. You can use this switch with any other MEM command switches.

- **/classify** (or **/c**) lists the memory below 1MB for each module, the amount of used and free memory, where DOS is loaded, the largest executable program size, and the largest free UMB (upper memory block).

- **/module** *pgmname* (or **/m** *pgmname*) returns the segment addresses, segment sizes, and the total size occupied by the program module specified by *pgmname.*

- **/free** (or **/f**) shows the amount of memory available.

- **/debug** (or **/d**) shows the status of all modules and internal drivers in memory. The report includes each module's size, segment address, and module type, as well as a summary of overall memory use.

Using MemMaker to Optimize Memory the Easy Way

If you have an 80386- or 80486-based system, you can optimize memory use with MemMaker, a new DOS 6 program. MemMaker analyzes your system's memory, figures out how to move memory-resident programs and device drivers to unused upper memory blocks, and changes your CONFIG.SYS and AUTOEXEC.BAT files to implement the optimized configuration each time you restart your computer.

80386 and 80486 optimization

After you run MemMaker, your computer's memory will remain optimized until you add or remove memory-resident programs or device drivers.

You should keep the following points in mind when working with MemMaker.

MemMaker guidelines

- After running MemMaker, *do not* alter any switches and options included with DEVICEHIGH, LOADHIGH, and EMM386 commands in CONFIG.SYS or AUTOEXEC.BAT.

- After updating CONFIG.SYS with new or deleted drivers, you should run MemMaker again.

- Windows and Windows-based applications need as much extended memory as they can get. Therefore, if you run those applications exclusively, you should either avoid using MemMaker or choose the Custom Setup option described later.

If MemMaker isn't appropriate for your system, you can use the commands DEVICEHIGH, LOADHIGH, HIMEM, and possibly EMM386 to make memory adjustments manually. For more information, see those entries in Help (for example, type **help devicehigh**).

Starting MemMaker

Before using MemMaker, close Windows and the DOS Shell, but make sure that you *are* running all devices and TSRs you want to optimize. Also be sure that you're logged onto the network, if you have one installed. Now, proceed as follows.

1. Type **memmaker** and press ↵.

2. Read the welcome screen, then press ↵ to continue.

3. The next screen allows you to choose between Express Setup (the default) or Custom Setup. To toggle between these selections, press the space bar. Generally, Express Setup will be just what you want. Press ↵ when you've made your choice.

Using Express Setup

After selecting Express Setup, follow these steps.

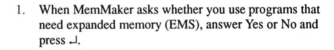

1. When MemMaker asks whether you use programs that need expanded memory (EMS), answer Yes or No and press ↵.

    If you do not have programs that require expanded memory, or you're not sure, leave the response set to No (the default). If you have programs that require expanded memory, press the space bar to change the response to Yes.

2. MemMaker will check for the presence of Microsoft Windows, then prompt you to remove disks from the floppy disk drives before it restarts your computer. Follow the instructions and press ↵ to restart your computer.

    If your computer doesn't restart properly, just turn it off and on again; MemMaker will recover automatically. If a program other than MemMaker starts after your computer restarts, exit the program normally so that MemMaker can continue.

3. Press ↵ when prompted to restart your computer with the new configuration that MemMaker determined.

4. When MemMaker asks you to confirm that the system works correctly, press ↵. (If there is a problem, consult your user's manual.)

5. After MemMaker displays a list of the new memory locations, press ↵ to exit the program and accept the changes. (If you want to undo the changes and restore your original system files, press Esc instead, then press **Y.**)

Using Custom Setup

Express Setup works well for most systems and is the easiest method to use. However, Custom Setup may help free more conventional memory and provide better optimization in the following situations:

When to use Custom Setup

*   You had problems with a device driver or program when you ran MemMaker, or your computer locked up.

*   You use an EGA or VGA monitor.

*   You don't run non-Windows applications with Windows.

To start MemMaker and run Custom Setup, type **memmaker** and press ↵. Press ↵ again to bypass the welcome screen, press the space bar to select Custom Setup from the second screen, and press ↵ once more. As with the Express Setup, you'll be asked whether you use programs that need expanded memory. Select No (the default) or press the space bar to answer Yes, then press ↵.

Next, the Advanced Options screen will present a list of items for you to answer with either Yes or No (see Figure 13.1). To select a different option, press the ↑ or ↓ key to highlight the option you want, then press the space bar to toggle the response between Yes and No. When you've finished making your selections, press ↵ to begin optimizing memory. MemMaker will carry out the same process and display the same prompts as for the Express Setup.

If your system crashes whenever you run MemMaker, try answering No to the question *Scan the upper memory area aggressively?* For more information about selections on the Advanced Options screen, press F1.

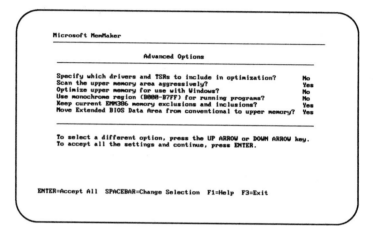

```
Microsoft MemMaker

                        Advanced Options

Specify which drivers and TSRs to include in optimization?    No
Scan the upper memory area aggressively?                      Yes
Optimize upper memory for use with Windows?                   No
Use monochrome region (B000-B7FF) for running programs?       No
Keep current EMM386 memory exclusions and inclusions?         Yes
Move Extended BIOS Data Area from conventional to upper memory? Yes


To select a different option, press the UP ARROW or DOWN ARROW key.
To accept all the settings and continue, press ENTER.




ENTER=Accept All   SPACEBAR=Change Selection   F1=Help   F3=Exit
```

Figure 13.1: MemMaker's Advanced Options screen

Undoing MemMaker's Memory Reconfiguration

You can restore your original memory configuration, if necessary. Quit all your programs and return to the command prompt. Then type **memmaker /undo** and press ↵. When prompted, press ↵ to undo the changes. MemMaker will restore your original CONFIG.SYS and AUTOEXEC.BAT files and restart your computer.

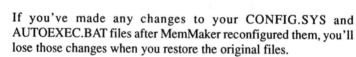

If you've made any changes to your CONFIG.SYS and AUTOEXEC.BAT files after MemMaker reconfigured them, you'll lose those changes when you restore the original files.

Protection from Viruses

Viruses are programs that are silently installed on your computer for the sole purpose of disrupting its operations. In this step, you'll learn how to use DOS 6 features that help you guard against, detect, and eradicate viruses.

Understanding Computer Viruses

Some viruses are merely mischievous, while others can destroy your programs, your data, or both. The main types of viruses are listed below.

Types of viruses

- *Boot sector viruses* replace the portion of the disk that controls the operating system startup, then spread from disk to disk.

- *File infectors* add on to executable files, so that they are activated when the file is run, then spread to program files.

- *Trojan horses* seem to be ordinary programs, but damage or destroy files and disks.

Monitoring Your Computer for Viruses

VSAFE is a memory-resident program that guards your system against viruses and displays a warning if it identifies one. VSAFE is available for both MS-DOS and Windows, depending on choices you make when installing DOS 6. I'll describe the DOS version here.

Loading VSAFE for DOS

To load VSAFE into memory, type **vsafe** and press ↵ at the command prompt.

Configuring VSAFE for DOS

You can change VSAFE options after you load the program. Simply press the *hot key* Alt+V to open the VSAFE pop-up menu. When the menu appears, type the number of the option you want to change. Each time you select an option, it will either be turned on (an X will appear next to it) or off (the X will be cleared). The following options are available.

- **1** Warns you about formatting that could erase the hard disk; the default setting is on.

- **2** Warns you if a program is trying to stay resident in memory; the default setting is off.

- **3** Prevents programs from writing to the disk; the default setting is off.

- **4** Checks executable files as they are opened; the default setting is on.

- **5** Checks all disks for boot sector viruses; the default setting is on.

- **6** Warns of attempts to change the hard disk's boot sector or partition table; the default setting is on.

- **7** Warns of attempts to write to a floppy disk's boot sector; the default setting is off.

- **8** Warns of attempts to modify executable files; the default setting is off.

Press Esc to clear the pop-up menu.

Note: You also can supply VSAFE options on the command line. Type **help vsafe** for details.

Removing Vsafe from Memory

To remove VSAFE from memory, type **vsafe /u** and press ↵, or press Alt+V then Alt+U.

Scanning Disks for Viruses

Microsoft Anti-Virus, or MSAV, is a program you should run peri-
odically to search for over 1000 specific viruses. If MSAV finds a
virus, you can direct the program to clean, or *disinfect*, the disk. You
also can use the program to learn more about the listed viruses. As
with VSAFE, DOS 6 includes versions of Anti-Virus for DOS and
Windows. I'll discuss only the DOS version here.

*Finding
existing
viruses*

Note: Microsoft Anti-Virus is licensed from Central Point Software,
and you can order updates of the list of viruses from that company.
See your DOS manual for ordering information.

You can run Anti-Virus interactively, or add it to your AUTO-
EXEC.BAT file so that it runs automatically whenever you start up
your system.

Running Anti-Virus Interactively

To run Anti-Virus interactively, type **msav** and press ↵ at the
command prompt. When the Main Menu appears, you can select
any of the options listed below.

- **Detect** scans the entire current work drive (usually
  drive C), reports any viruses found, and lets you remove
  them.

- **Detect & Clean** has the same effect as Detect but removes
  viruses automatically.

- **Select New Drive** allows you to select a different drive;
  use the arrow keys to highlight the drive and press ↵, or
  click on the drive you want.

- **Options** allows you to exercise more control over
  Microsoft Anti-Virus's behavior.

- **Exit** allows you to save configuration options and exit
  to DOS.

To select an option, highlight it with the arrow keys and press ↵, or
press (or click) one of the function keys listed on the status line at

the bottom of the screen. The function keys are F1=Help, F2=Select New Drive, F3=Exit, F4=Detect, F5=Detect & Clean, F7=Delete checklist files from the current drive, F8=Options, and F9=List (described later in this Step).

Running Anti-Virus Automatically

To run Anti-Virus whenever you restart the computer, place the MSAV command in your AUTOEXEC.BAT file and specify the drives and command line switches you want to use (type **help msav** for a complete list of switches). For example, the command line **msav c: d:** /c /p runs Anti-Virus on drives C and D, removes any viruses detected (the /c switch), and does not use the graphical display during scanning (the /p switch).

If your computer is connected to a network, add the switch /l to confine the scan to local drives.

Getting Information about Detectable Viruses

To learn more about any of the viruses that Anti-Virus can detect, start Anti-Virus and press F9 when the Main Menu appears. Use the arrow keys to highlight the virus name and press ↵. Alternatively, you can click on the name with your mouse, or type the virus name (or partial name) and press ↵. After viewing the virus information, press ↵ to clear the message. Press Esc to return to the Main Menu screen.

DOS 6 includes two programs, named INTERLNK and INTERSVR, that let you connect two computers without expensive networking equipment. Once you've connected them via cable, you can easily move or copy files from one computer to the other, without using floppies. These programs are particularly handy when you want to transfer files between a laptop and a desktop computer.

Client and Server

When you link two computers with INTERLNK, the computer you use to type commands is called the *client*. The computer connected to the client is the *server*. It usually doesn't matter, however, which computer is which. If one of the two computers has a better keyboard, use that one as the client.

INTERLNK Hardware Requirements

You don't need any fancy network cards or special hardware to use INTERLNK. But you do need a cable to connect the two computers. You can use either the parallel printer ports or the serial ports of the two computers. For a parallel connection, you need a bidirectional parallel cable. For a serial connection, you need either a 3-wire serial cable or a 7-wire null-modem serial cable.

Be sure to connect the two computers before activating the INTERLNK and INTERSVR software. Otherwise, the software cannot recognize the connection.

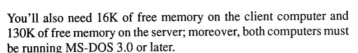

You'll also need 16K of free memory on the client computer and 130K of free memory on the server; moreover, both computers must be running MS-DOS 3.0 or later.

INTERLNK Software Requirements

It's not necessary for both computers to use DOS 6. However, the client computer must have INTERLNK.EXE on disk and the server computer must have INTERSVR.EXE. But there's no harm in having both programs on both computers. Both INTERLNK.EXE and INTERSVR.EXE are copied to the \DOS directory when you install DOS 6.

What If My Computer Has No Floppy?

Some computers, including palmtops, have no floppy disk. Fortunately, you can still copy INTERLNK.EXE and INTERSVR.EXE from any computer that has those files installed to a floppy-deprived machine. In the steps below, the floppy-less machine you're copying *to* is the *remote* computer.

The MODE command must be available on the remote computer.

1. Use a 7-wire null-modem serial cable to connect the computers. (Sorry, a 3-wire serial cable or parallel cable won't work.)

2. Disable SHARE.EXE on the remote computer. If that computer's AUTOEXEC.BAT file loads SHARE.EXE, use EDIT to remove the line or convert it to a comment (see Step 17). To convert a line to a comment, type **REM** followed by a space at the beginning of the line. Save your changes and reboot the remote computer.

3. On the computer you're copying *from*, type

   ```
   intersvr/rcopy
   ```

   at the command prompt.

4. Follow the instructions on the screen to copy the files INTERSVR.EXE and INTERLNK.EXE to the remote computer.

Making the Connection

When the cable is in place, and each computer has the appropriate programs available, here's how you make the connection (note that you only need to perform steps 1 – 4 once, not each time you wish to make a connection):

1. Start at the DOS command prompt on the client computer. Use EDIT (described in Step 17) to open the C:\CONFIG.SYS file.

2. Add the command **device=c:\dos\interlnk.exe**, on its own line, near the end of CONFIG.SYS. Optionally, if you want to choose whether to turn INTERLNK on or off each time you start your computer, put a question mark (?) in front of the equal sign like this: **device?=c:\dos\interlnk.exe** (see Step 18 for more information on the ? symbol).

3. Exit the editor and choose Yes to save your changes. You'll return to the DOS command prompt.

4. Reboot the client machine (press Ctrl+Alt+Del). You may notice a message indicating that no connection was made. Don't worry about that.

5. Go over to the server computer's keyboard, and enter the command **intersvr**.

6. Now go back to the client computer, and enter the command **interlnk**.

You'll see a description of how the client will treat drives on the server, as in Figure 15.1.

The screen is telling you that any reference to drive I on the current (client) computer really refers to drive A on the other (server) computer. Similarly, any reference to drive K that you make on this computer will actually be drive C on the other computer.

You now have complete control over the server computer from your current client computer's keyboard. Here are some examples of

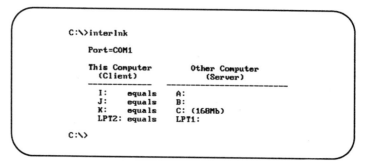

Figure 15.1: INTERLNK's drive-mapping display

ways you can view and transfer files (substitute appropriate commands and drive letters for your own computers, based on the information on your screen at the moment):

Examples

- Enter the command **tree k:** to view the directory tree of drive C on the server computer.

- Enter the command **copy k:\mydirec*.*** to copy all the files from C:\MYDIREC of the server computer to the current drive and directory of the client computer.

- Enter **copy c:\mydirec*.* k:\mydirec*.*** to copy all the files from the C:\MYDIREC directory of the current (client) computer to the C:\MYDIREC directory of the other (server) computer.

- Enter **echo ^L >lpt2:** (where you press Ctrl+L to type ^L) to eject a page from the printer attached to LPT1 on the server computer.

You can even go into the DOS Shell and copy and move files between computers with simple dragging.

Just remember that all the drive letters on the server computer are "larger" now. For example, drive A on the server will now be treated as drive I (or whatever). Just look to the server's screen, or enter the command **interlnk** at the command prompt on the client computer, when you need a reminder about which drive letter is which.

Accessing More than Three Server Drives

You probably noticed that Figure 15.1 showed only three drives—A, B, and C—available on the server. By default, INTERLNK.EXE allows the client computer to use only three server drives. However, you can easily increase the number of drives available. To do this, add the /DRIVES switch to the DEVICE= line in CONFIG.SYS. The general form of this switch is /DRIVES:*n* (where *n* is the number of drives the client computer can use on the server).

Suppose your server has two floppy drives (A and) and two hard drives (C and D). The simple DEVICE= command shown earlier will let you use drives A, B, and C on the server, but *not* drive D. To solve this problem, open the client computer's CONFIG.SYS file in the Editor. Now add the /DRIVES switch to the DEVICE= command for INTERLNK, like this:

```
device=c:\dos\interlnk.exe /drives:4
```

The /DRIVES switch in this example will let the client access four drives on the server. Now, exit the Editor, save your changes, and reboot the client computer. The next time you type **interlnk** at the command prompt, you'll see the additional server drive included in the list of available drives.

Commands to Avoid During a Link

The following DOS commands don't work with INTERLNK: CHKDSK, DEFRAG, DISKCOMP, DISKCOPY, FDISK, FORMAT, MIRROR, SYS, UNDELETE, and UNFORMAT. You should also avoid task swapping in the Shell (and Windows) while you're in an INTERLNK connection.

Breaking the Connection

To break the INTERLNK connection between computers, press Alt+F4 on the server's keyboard. To restart the server, type **intersvr** at the server's command prompt.

Troubleshooting

If you have a problem, first make sure the computers are connected correctly and you've started the server. If you're OK there, make sure the LASTDRIVE= command in each computer's CONFIG.SYS file is set high enough to accommodate all the drive names. For example, if each computer has four drives, A through D, then you need to have eight drive names available, A, B, C, D, E, F, G, and H. Thus, the appropriate command in each computer's CONFIG.SYS file would be

```
lastdrive=h
```

When in doubt, err on the side of setting LASTDRIVE too high. For example, there's no harm in using the command **lastdrive=n** rather than **lastdrive=h** in CONFIG.SYS. And don't forget that after changing and saving the CONFIG.SYS file, you still need to reboot to activate the new LASTDRIVE command.

If you aren't using a network, simply omit the LASTDRIVE command. DOS will set the default LASTDRIVE value to the letter following the last one in use.

You shouldn't change or delete the LASTDRIVE command when the client computer is connected to a Novell network. That's because Novell network drives start with the letter *after* the drive specified by LASTDRIVE. Different LASTDRIVE settings might cause problems with batch programs and other commands that rely on a particular drive letter. Moreover, a LASTDRIVE that's too high may prevent you from using your network drives at all.

Server drives are not ready

If you try to access a drive on the server computer from the Shell or Windows File Manager, and DOS reports a "Not ready" error on that drive, chances are you've just forgotten to run INTERSVR. Go to the server computer's keyboard and enter the command **intersvr** so that you see the INTERSVR screen. Then go back over to the client computer's keyboard and try again. If the server's floppy drive is "Not ready," make sure that it contains a properly inserted disk.

For More Info

For more information on INTERLNK, INTERSVR, optional parameters and switches, and cabling, enter **help interlnk** or **help interlnk.exe** or **help intersvr** at the DOS command prompt.

Conserving Laptop Battery Power

You can use DOS 6's new POWER command to extend your laptop computer's battery life by 5% to 25%. The amount of extra life depends on how the computer manages power, with the greatest savings for computers that conform to the Advanced Power Management (APM) specification. Check your laptop's documentation to see whether the specification applies.

Loading the Device Driver

Before you can use POWER, the POWER.EXE device driver must be loaded into memory. To do this, add the appropriate DEVICE command to your CONFIG.SYS file. You can use EDIT (described in Step 17) to edit C:\CONFIG.SYS. (If you boot from a floppy, edit A:\CONFIG.SYS on that bootable floppy.)

Insert, on its own line, a DEVICE= command followed by the location and name of the POWER program. Assuming POWER is on the \DOS directory, you'd add this command to your CONFIG.SYS file:

```
device=c:\dos\power.exe
```

Save your changes to CONFIG.SYS, return to the command prompt, and restart your computer. Each time you start the computer in the future, the POWER driver will load automatically.

Displaying and Changing Power Settings

Once you've loaded POWER.EXE via CONFIG.SYS, you can view or change your current power status. Starting at the DOS command prompt, type **power** and press ↵ to view the current status.

To change the power setting, follow the POWER command with a space and the appropriate parameter, as described here:

- To conserve power while programs and hardware are idle, use the parameter ADV. You can follow the parameter with a colon (:) and one of these settings: MAX (for maximum power conservation), REG (for regular power conservation), or MIN (for minimum power conservation). The default setting, ADV:REG or just ADV, balances power conservation with program and hardware performance. The setting ADV:MAX provides maximum power conservation but may slow performance. Use POWER ADV:MIN if performance suffers with the ADV:MAX or ADV:REG settings.

- To use the hardware power management features of an APM computer, type **power std**. If you use the STD parameter on a non-APM computer, you'll turn off power management.

- To turn power management off, type **power off**.

Default power setting

You can choose a default power setting by adding the appropriate parameter to the **device=c:\dos\power.exe** command in your CONFIG.SYS file. For example, if your CONFIG.SYS file contains this command:

```
device=c:\dos\power.exe adv:max
```

your laptop will always start up with maximum power conservation. You can override that setting by typing the POWER command at the command prompt.

For More Information

For more information and options, enter **help power.exe** or **help power** at the command prompt. Also, refer to the user's manual for your laptop computer.

Editing Text Files

30

The EDIT text editor that comes with DOS 5 and 6 provides a simple way to create, edit, and print text (ASCII) files. Common text files include CONFIG.SYS, AUTOEXEC.BAT, Windows initialization files (.INI), and batch programs that you write. You can use EDIT to customize these text files and control your computer in powerful ways.

Most word processors can also edit text files. If you'd rather use your favorite word processor to edit text files, that's fine. However, be sure to save those text files in ASCII format, and *not* in "word processor" format. You can ruin a text file and make it useless to DOS or Windows if you save it in word processor format.

Your computer reads the file CONFIG.SYS when you first turn it on. This file contains information on how to configure your system. Next, it reads the file AUTOEXEC.BAT, which contains "regular" DOS commands that execute before you see the DOS prompt. Both files are on the root directory of your startup drive—typically, C:\.

When you install new hardware or programs, the installation procedure usually updates CONFIG.SYS and AUTOEXEC.BAT automatically. So you'll rarely need to change those files yourself. But when you do need to edit those files, you can use the techniques discussed in this step.

CONFIG.SYS, AUTOEXEC.BAT, and initialization files contain information that's crucial to the proper functioning of your computer. Don't "experiment" with EDIT by playing around with any of those important files. If you want to experiment, do so with a "junk" file (perhaps named JUNK.TXT) rather than an important file.

Starting EDIT

To start EDIT from the Shell,

1. Select Editor from the Main group in the Program List (double-click or highlight it and press ↵).

2. When prompted, type the path and name of the file you want to edit (e.g. **C:\AUTOEXEC.BAT**) then press ↵ or click OK.

Or, if you are working from the command prompt

• Enter the EDIT command followed by the path and name of the file you want to edit, for example:

```
edit c:\autoexec.bat
```

You can omit the file name in either method above. This will start EDIT with a dialog box that asks whether you want to see the Survival Guide. Press ↵ to see this online help system or press Escape (Esc) to go straight into editing.

Empty
Files

People sometimes forget to include the drive and directory when typing the name of an existing file they want to edit. This causes the editor to create a new, blank file on the current directory. To correct the problem, you can choose File ⇒ Open from the menus, type the complete drive, directory, and file name, and then press ↵. Or just exit the editor (choose File ⇒ Exit) and try again.

Getting Around the Editor

Once you're in the editor, the main keys you'll use are:

• **Alt**: Activates the menu bar (select menu commands with the usual arrow keys and ↵, or your mouse).

• **F1**: Opens the online Survival Guide help system. Selectable topics are displayed between < and > symbols. To select a topic, double-click it with your mouse or move the cursor to it by pressing Tab or Shift+Tab, and then ↵. The status bar at the bottom of the screen shows other keys you can use.

- **Esc**: Backs out of the current window, help screen, or dialog box without making a selection.

- **Mouse button**: Click any menu option to select it. You can also click a key definition in the status bar. For example, click <F1=Help> to get help.

Typing

To type in the editor, just type as you normally would. Press ↵ at the end of each line. (Unlike a word processing program, EDIT offers no automatic "word wrap," since it's not designed to work with paragraphs. Each line can have up to 256 characters.)

Editing

Table 17.1 lists keys for moving the cursor and scrolling text. These keys work *only* with existing text. To move to the right when there is no existing text, press the space bar, not →. To move down to a new line if you're at the end of a file, press ↵, not ↓.

Notice that some keystrokes shown in Table 17.1 require you to press two or more key combinations. For example, to move the cursor to the top of the screen, you press Ctrl+Q, E. This means "Hold down the Ctrl key and tap the Q key. Now release the Ctrl key and tap the E key."

Key	*Purpose*
Mouse click	Move cursor to mouse pointer
↑, ↓, ←, →	Move one character or line at a time
Ctrl+←	Move left one word
Ctrl+→	Move right one word
Home	Move to start of line

Table 17.1: Keys for Moving the Cursor in EDIT

Key	Purpose
End	Move to end of line
Page Up	Move up a screen
Page Down	Move down a screen
Ctrl+⤶	Move to start of next line
Ctrl+Q, E	Move to top of screen
Ctrl+Q, X	Move to bottom of screen
Ctrl+Home or Ctrl+Q, R	Move to the top of the file
Ctrl+End or Ctrl+Q, C	Move to the bottom of the file
Ctrl+W or Ctrl+↑	Scroll up a line
Ctrl+Z or Ctrl+↓	Scroll down a line
Ctrl+Page Up	Scroll to the right one screen
Ctrl+Page Down	Scroll to the left one screen

Table 17.1: Keys for Moving the Cursor in EDIT (continued)

You can also use the scroll bars at the right and bottom of the editing window to scroll through a file. Table 17.2 lists the basic keys for changing text.

Key	Purpose
Backspace or Ctrl+H	Delete character to left of cursor
Delete or Ctrl+G	Delete character at the cursor
Ctrl+T	Delete from the cursor to the end of the word
Insert or Ctrl+V	Switch between Insert and Overwrite modes
Ctrl+Y	Delete entire line
Ctrl+Q, Y	Delete from cursor to end of line

Table 17.2: Basic Editing Keys Used in EDIT

To get a quick reminder about useful keys, choose Help ⇒ Keyboard from the main menu bar.

Inserting a New Line

Here's how to insert a new line between existing lines in a file. First use the arrow and End keys to move the cursor to the end of the line that's above where you want to type a new line. Then press ↲.

Selecting Blocks

Text selection is one of the best features of a screen editor. This feature lets you select any block of text (by highlighting it), and then move, copy, or delete it. To select a block of text with your mouse:

1. Move the mouse pointer to the first character of text you want to select.

2. Drag to the last character that you want to select.

3. Release the mouse button.

Mouse

If you change your mind or want to re-select, first click anywhere on the EDIT screen to unselect.

To select a block with your keyboard:

1. Move the cursor to the first character of text you want to select.

2. Hold down the Shift key and then use the arrow keys to move the cursor to the last character you want to select.

3. Release the keys.

Keyboard

If you want to cancel the selection, press any arrow key or Esc.

Moving Selected Text

To move the currently selected text:

1. Select Edit ⇒ Cut, or press Shift+Delete. (EDIT removes the selected text and hides it in the Clipboard.)
2. Place the cursor where you want to move the hidden text.
3. Select Edit ⇒ Paste, or press Shift+Ins.

Copying Selected Text

To copy (duplicate) the selected text somewhere else:

1. Select Edit ⇒ Copy, or press Ctrl+Insert.
2. Place the cursor where you want the copied text to appear.
3. Select Edit ⇒ Paste, or press Ctrl+Insert.

Deleting Selected Text

To delete the currently selected text:

*   Select Edit ⇒ Clear, or press Del.

Finding Text

To locate a particular word or phrase in your text file,

1. Place the cursor where you want to begin the search (EDIT starts searching below the current cursor position).
2. Select Search ⇒ Find.
3. Type the text you want to search for, then press Tab.
4. If you want to find only text with matching upper/ lowercase letters, check that box.

5. If you want to find only whole-word matches (for example, to ignore *actress* when you're looking for *act*) check the Whole Word box.

6. Select OK.

7. If you want to continue the same search, select Search ⇒ Repeat Last Find, or press F3, until you find the exact item you're looking for.

Replacing Text

To replace a particular word or phrase throughout your document,

1. Place the cursor where you want to start replacing text.

2. Select Search ⇒ Change.

3. Type the text you want to replace, then press Tab.

4. Type the new text (or leave this box blank if you want to delete the old text throughout the document), then press Tab.

5. Check Match Upper/Lowercase if you want to replace only text with the same case.

6. Check Whole Word if you want to replace matching whole words only.

7. If you want to double-check each replacement before it occurs, select Find and Verify. Otherwise, select Change All.

If you selected Find and Verify, you'll be prompted to Change or Skip the text each time EDIT finds a match. When you're done, select OK from the Change Complete dialog box that appears.

You can select text from the edit screen before starting the search or replacement. The selected text will automatically appear as the search text in the dialog box.

Typing Special Characters

To type a control (Ctrl) or other special character,

1. Turn on your keyboard's Num Lock key.

2. Position the cursor where you want to type the special character.

3. Press Ctrl+P.

4. Hold down the Alt key and type the character's three-digit ASCII number on the numeric keypad (don't use the number keys at the top of the keyboard). Release the Alt key after typing the number.

Remember to turn Num Lock off again if you want to use the arrow and other special keys on the numeric keypad.

A Page-
Eject Macro

Suppose you want to create a macro that ejects the page from the printer when you enter the command **ff** (an abbreviation for "form feed"). To accomplish that, you need the macro to send a Ctrl+L to the printer. Since L is the 12th letter of the alphabet, a Ctrl+L is ASCII character 012. Thus, in your AUTOEXEC.BAT file, you'd add this line:

```
doskey ff=echo ♀ $g prn
```

To type the Ctrl+L, which appears as the female symbol, you first press Ctrl+P. Then hold down the Alt key, and type 012 on the numeric keypad. Release the Alt key. The female symbol should appear. (If it doesn't work, press Num Lock and then try again.)

In the future, DOS will create the FF macro each time you start your computer. So when you're at the command prompt, you just enter the command **ff** rather than **echo ^L >prn** when you want to eject a page. Very convenient (albeit a bit nerdy). To learn more about DOSKEY and DOS macros, you can look at DOSKEY in your online documentation.

Printing the File

To print all (or some) of the file you're editing,

1. If you want to print only a portion of the text, select that text.

2. Select File $\Rightarrow$ Print.

3. If prompted, choose either Selected Text Only or Complete Document, whichever you want to print.

4. Select OK.

Changing Screen Colors

To change the colors on the Editor screen,

1. Select Options $\Rightarrow$ Display.

2. Select a foreground and background color from the dialog box that appears (or press F1 if you need help).

3. Select OK.

Saving and Exiting

The File menu provides several options that let you save your document, and either stay in the Editor or leave it:

- **New**: Lets you save the current file (if you wish), then clears it from the screen. Now you can start typing new text.

- **Open**: Lets you select a new file to open; if the current file has not been saved, prompts you to save it.

- **Save**: Saves the current file and leaves it on the screen.

- **Save As**: Lets you give a new name to the current version of the file so that the original file remains unchanged.

- **Exit**: Lets you save the current file (if any), then exits to the command prompt or Shell.

When you save a file with a new name, you can just type the drive and directory name. Or you can select a disk drive and directory from the dialog box that appears (or select [..] to move up a level in the directory tree). If you do not specify a drive and directory, EDIT uses the current drive and directory. If you do not specify a file name, the file is named Untitled. EDIT will overwrite the Untitled file the next time you save an unnamed file.

Exiting the Editor

To return to the Shell or command prompt:

1. Select File $\Rightarrow$ Exit.

2. If the current file is new or you've changed it but haven't saved it yet, select Yes to save it now, or No to abandon recent changes.

If Nothing Seems to Happen...

Remember that any changes you make to AUTOEXEC.BAT or CONFIG.SYS won't take effect until the next time you start your computer or reboot using Ctrl+Alt+Del. Similarly, any changes you make to an initialization (.INI) file won't have any effect until the next time you start the program that reads the initialization file.

Creating Startup Configurations

It's not uncommon for several people who share a single computer to have different needs and startup requirements. DOS 6 offers four new commands—MENUITEM, MENUDEFAULT, MENUCOLOR, and SUBMENU—that you can use to write alternative configurations in the CONFIG.SYS file. These commands let users select a configuration from a menu at startup.

To take advantage of the flexibility these menuing commands provide, you should understand the contents of a CONFIG.SYS file—a topic this book doesn't have room to cover in detail.

If you're an aspiring techno-nerd, and want to learn more about CONFIG.SYS, you can get started via the online documentation. Enter **help config** at the command prompt.

Providing Multiple Startup Configurations

To define multiple configurations in CONFIG.SYS, you need to:

- Define a main menu at the top of CONFIG.SYS, using the [menu] identifier and MENUITEM commands. Users will select one option from this menu to choose the configuration they need.

- Create a configuration block for each configuration. Each block starts with a name surrounded by square brackets ([ ]) and contains suitable commands to configure the system. Each menu block name corresponds to an option in the main menu.

You can use the DOS Editor, described in Step 17, to change the C:\CONFIG.SYS file.

Defining the Configuration Menu

To define the main menu, type the command [menu] at the top of the CONFIG.SYS file. Beneath that, add one MENUITEM command for each option that you want the menu to show. For example, this sequence of commands in CONFIG.SYS defines three main menu items: Windows, DOS, and Network:

```
[menu]
menuitem=Windows
menuitem=DOS
menuitem=Network
```

You can also add descriptive menu text to each definition, such as **menuitem=Windows,Windows configuration**. In this case, *Windows configuration* appears on the screen at startup, but **Windows** is the name you use in later commands that define the Windows configuration block.

Creating the Configuration Blocks

After you've defined your menu, create a configuration block for each menu item. Begin each block with the block name enclosed in square brackets. Be sure to use the name you defined in the MENUITEM command. Then press ⏎ and type the configuration commands for that item.

For example, the commands below show a sample configuration file for the Windows, DOS, and Network options. Notice that the name of each block is the same as defined in the MENUITEM commands:

```
[menu]
menuitem=Windows
menuitem=DOS
menuitem=Network
[Windows]
set path=c:\dos\windows;c:\dos
set temp=c:\windows\temp
```

```
[DOS]
set path=c:\dos
device=c:\dos\emm386
[Network]
device=c:\net\net.sys
set path=c:\dos;c:\network
```

You must create a configuration block for each MENUITEM command. If any MENUITEM command has no configuration block, DOS reports an error in CONFIG.SYS at startup.

DOS stores the name of the configuration item the user selects from the menu in an environmental variable named CONFIG. You can use that variable in AUTOEXEC and other batch files, as you'll see in the next Step.

Defining Universal Configuration Commands

You might also want your CONFIG.SYS file to contain commands that execute regardless of which option the user chooses. You can include these under the block heading [common]. (Do not define a "common" option in [menu].) For example, you may want to load HIMEM, and load DOS high, regardless of which configuration the user selects. In that case, you could just add this configuration block to the CONFIG.SYS file:

```
[common]
device=c:\dos\himem.sys
dos=high
```

You should end your CONFIG.SYS file with an empty [common] block, because some installation programs may need it when they add commands automatically.

Including One Menu Block in Another

The command INCLUDE lets you include one menu block in another. For example, to include the DOS block in the Network block, you would add the command **include=DOS** to the [Network] block.

Setting the Num Lock Key On or Off

You can also turn Num Lock (number lock) on or off at startup. Use **numlock=on** to turn Num Lock on, or **numlock=off** to turn it off within a configuration block. When Num Lock is on, the numeric keypad types numbers. When it's off, the keypad's keys move the cursor.

Specifying a Default Menu Selection

The optional MENUDEFAULT command lets you specify a default configuration to load if a user doesn't make a menu selection within a given time period. Add the command **menudefault=** followed by the name of the configuration block, and the number of seconds you want to wait before DOS chooses the block automatically. Make it the last command in the [menu] block of the CONFIG.SYS file. For example, to use the Windows configuration if the user does not make a choice within 15 seconds, add this command beneath the last MENUITEM command in the [menu] block:

```
menudefault=Windows,15
```

Coloring the Menu

If your computer has a color monitor, you can use the MENUCOLOR command within the [menu] block to specify the menu's text and background colors. For example, to specify bright white (number 12) text on a blue (number 1) background in the [menu] block, add the line

```
menucolor=15,1
```

to the bottom of the block. The numeric codes that you can use for colors in the **menucolor=** command are:

0	Black
1	Blue
2	Green
3	Cyan
4	Red
5	Magenta
6	Brown
7	White
8	Gray
9	Bright blue
10	Bright green
11	Bright cyan
12	Bright red
13	Bright magenta
14	Yellow
15	Bright white

Colors 8 through 15 will blink on some monitors.

A Sample CONFIG.SYS File

The lines that follow show a complete CONFIG.SYS file after adding multiple configuration commands to it.

```
[menu]
menuitem=Windows,Windows configuration
menuitem=DOS,DOS configuration
menuitem=network,Network configuration
menudefault=Windows,15
menucolor=12,14
```

```
[common]
device=c:\dos\himem.sys
dos=high
files=40

[Windows]
set path=c:\dos\windows;c:\dos
set temp=c:\windows\temp
numlock=off

[DOS]
set path=c:\dos
device=c:\dos\emm386
numlock=on

[Network]
device=c:\net\net.sys
set path=c:\dos;c:\network
include=DOS


[common]
```

When you start the computer with this CONFIG.SYS file, the screen will display:

```
1. Windows configuration
2. DOS configuration
3. Network configuration


Enter a choice:
```

The user has 15 seconds to make a choice, either 1, 2, or 3. Once the user makes a choice, DOS executes the [common] block; then it executes only the commands in the appropriate configuration block. If no choice is made within 15 seconds, DOS runs the commands in the [common] and [Windows] blocks by default, because of the MENUDEFAULT command.

Two other options—F5 and F8—will appear at the bottom of the screen if you've defined a [menu] block in CONFIG.SYS. You can press F5 to bypass the CONFIG.SYS and AUTOEXEC.BAT commands completely. Or press F8 to choose exactly which CONFIG.SYS commands you want to run and decide whether to run AUTOEXEC.BAT. See "Bypassing Configuration Commands" later in this Step.

Creating a Submenu

Only nine options are allowed on a menu. You can get around this limit and display a submenu by using the SUBMENU command. For more information and examples, see SUBMENU in the online documentation (enter **help submenu**). You can also enter **help multi-config** for more general information and examples.

Comments and Questions in CONFIG.SYS

DOS 6 also lets you use two new characters in CONFIG.SYS:

;   Treats the command as a comment so it won't be executed (same as the REM command). Always place the semicolon at the beginning of the line.

?   Always prompts for permission before executing the command at startup. Always place the question mark just before the equal sign in the command.

For example, in this series of CONFIG.SYS commands:

```
;Load multimedia device drivers,
;if user approves.
device?=c:\proaudio\mvsound.sys d:3 q:5
device?=c:\proaudio\sony_pfm.sys /d:mvcd001
```

the first line acts only as a reminder about the purpose of the commands that follow. The next two lines will appear on the screen at startup, followed by [Y,N] options. They'll be executed only if the user types a Y (or y) in response to the [Y,N] prompt.

Bypassing Configuration Commands

DOS 6 lets you bypass configuration commands on-the-fly during startup. This is particularly handy for troubleshooting faulty configurations. To bypass commands, start your computer normally, or reboot using Ctrl+Alt+Del. Then...

- If you want to bypass *all* the commands in CONFIG.SYS and AUTOEXEC.BAT, press the F5 key just after the *Starting MS-DOS...* message appears.

- If you want to bypass only specific CONFIG.SYS commands, press F8 just after the *Starting MS-DOS...* message appears. Then answer Y or N as the screen asks whether to process each command. You'll also be given a chance to execute all, or none, of the commands in AUTOEXEC.BAT.

Passing the Configuration Choice to Other Programs

If your CONFIG.SYS file contains a menu block, DOS will automatically create an environmental variable named CONFIG at startup. That environmental variable contains the name of the configuration you selected.

At the command prompt, you can enter the command **set** to view the CONFIG (and all other) environmental variables. As we'll discuss in the next Step, you can use the variable name %CONFIG% in a batch program, including AUTOEXEC.BAT, to make decisions based on the contents of the CONFIG environmental variable.

A batch program (also called a batch file) is a collection of DOS commands stored in a text file, with the file name extension .BAT. For example, you might name a batch program HELLO.BAT. You can use EDIT, or any other text editor, to create a batch program.

After you create and save a batch program, you can run it like any other program, using the techniques discussed in Step 5. For example, after creating and saving a batch program named HELLO.BAT, you could type **hello** and then press ↵ at the command prompt to run that batch program. DOS will execute instructions in the batch program, just as though you had typed each command independently at the command prompt.

As with any program, if the batch program isn't located on the current directory, or one of the directories included in your PATH statement, you'll just get a *Bad command...* error message.

Like the CONFIG.SYS topic, batch programming is a much larger subject than this book has room to cover in depth. So I'll assume that you've already had a chance to create and use some batch programs.

Batch Programmers Now Have a CHOICE

One thing that's always been missing from DOS batch programs has been the ability to give users a set of options, then respond to the choice. DOS 6 finally has filled that gap with the new CHOICE command.

The general syntax for CHOICE is

```
choice [/c:keys] [/t:c,nn] [text]
```

where *keys* represents acceptable keystrokes the user can type. The /t switch imposes a time limit, choosing option *c* if the user doesn't respond within *nn* seconds. The *text* is the prompt that should appear on the screen.

The user's response to the prompt is stored as a numeric exit code, which reflects that option's position in the /c list. You can then use the IF ERRORLEVEL command to test the exit code returned. For instance, suppose the batch program contains the **choice/c:xyz** command. When that command runs, ERRORLEVEL will equal 1 if the user types **x**. If the user types **y**, ERRORLEVEL will contain 2, and so forth. (Not the most elegant way of doing things, but it works.)

For example, let's suppose you want to create a batch program that presents a simple menu of program options, like this:

```
1. WordPerfect
2. Lotus 123
3. Paradox
4. DOS Shell
5. DOS Command Prompt
Enter your choice [1,2,3,4,5]?
```

You then want the batch program to run whichever program you choose.

Let's further suppose that you decide to name this batch program MENU.BAT, and place it on the C:\DOS directory. (Because C:\DOS is in the PATH, the batch program will be accessible from any directory.)

So to get started, you need to enter **edit c:\dos\menu.bat** at the command prompt. Then you'd type in the appropriate commands, as in this example:

```
rem *************************** Menu.bat
rem ******* Display options to the user
:top
@echo off
cls
```

```
echo.
echo    1. WordPerfect
echo.
echo    2. Lotus 123
echo.
echo    3. Paradox
echo.
echo    4. DOS Shell
echo.
echo    5. DOS Command Prompt
echo.
choice /c:12345 /t:5,15 "  Enter your choice "


rem ********** Branch based on user's choice.
rem ** Always go from largest to smallest
rem ** ERRORLEVEL.
if ERRORLEVEL 5 goto Done
if ERRORLEVEL 4 goto DosShell
if ERRORLEVEL 3 goto Pdox
if ERRORLEVEL 2 goto 123
if ERRORLEVEL 1 goto wp


rem ** Sections referred to in the ERRORLEVEL
rem ** commands.
:wp
cd\wp51
wp
goto top


:123
cd\123
123
goto top


:Pdox
cd\paradox
```

```
paradox
goto top

:DosShell
cd\dos
dosshell
goto top

:Done
cls
echo Enter MENU to get back to the menu.
echo.
```

To better understand this batch program, let's look at the individual parts:

- The REM commands are just comments, and can be omitted.

- The CLS and ECHO commands clear the screen and display the menu. The ECHO. (echo dot) commands display a blank line.

- The CHOICE command defines the numbers 1, 2, 3, 4, and 5 as valid entries. The /t switch says "If you don't make a choice within 15 seconds, assume you chose 5." The text at the end of the CHOICE command is the prompt that will appear on the screen.

- The IF ERRORLEVEL commands pass control to some section of the batch program, based on the response to the CHOICE command's prompt. *These commands must appear in largest-to-smallest ERRORLEVEL order.* That's because, contrary to what you might assume, "if ERRORLEVEL" means "if ERRORLEVEL is greater than or equal to"—not "if ERRORLEVEL equals."

- The commands starting with a colon (:) are labels, where GOTO commands pass control. Notice that there's a corresponding label for each GOTO command in the batch program.

For instance, if you type **1** in response to the menu, the **if ERRORLEVEL 1 goto wp** command passes control to the label :wp. The next two commands switch to the WP51 directory and start the WordPerfect program. At that point, DOS and the batch program are suspended until you exit WordPerfect. When you do exit, the **goto top** command runs and redisplays the menu automatically.

For more information and examples, look up BATCH or CHOICE in the online documentation (enter **help batch** or **help choice** at the command prompt).

AUTOEXEC.BAT: A Special Batch Program

When you first start your computer, DOS locates and executes all the commands in CONFIG.SYS. Then, it looks for a file named AUTOEXEC.BAT on the root directory of the current drive. If it finds that file, it executes all the commands there before displaying the command prompt to you.

Like CONFIG.SYS, the AUTOEXEC.BAT file must be on the root directory of the startup drive (typically C:\); and you can change it with the DOS Editor. To do so, type **edit c:\autoexec.bat** at the command prompt. Unlike CONFIG.SYS, which can contain only certain commands, AUTOEXEC.BAT can contain virtually any DOS command.

Unfortunately, space doesn't permit me to go into all the details of AUTOEXEC.BAT here. Therefore, I'll just focus on what's new in DOS 6, and what's particularly important to know about AUTOEXEC.BAT.

Creating Multiple AUTOEXEC Configurations

Step 18 explained how DOS 6 stores your selection from a CONFIG.SYS startup menu in an environmental variable named CONFIG. You can create labels within your AUTOEXEC.BAT file that have the same names as corresponding configuration blocks in CONFIG.SYS. Then use GOTO to branch to the appropriate label.

Chances are, you'll want to execute some commands in AUTOEXEC.BAT regardless of the startup configuration you choose. List those commands first in AUTOEXEC.BAT. Then you can follow those commands with a **goto %config%** command, which branches control to a label in AUTOEXEC.BAT that has the same name as the corresponding configuration block in CONFIG.SYS.

Here's a sample AUTOEXEC.BAT file that executes the PATH, PROMPT, and MOUSE commands, regardless of what you selected from CONFIG.SYS. After executing those commands, the **goto %config%** command passes control to a label named DOS, Windows, or Network, depending on the contents of the CONFIG environmental variable. That variable will have been defined in CONFIG.SYS already, because CONFIG.SYS always runs before AUTOEXEC.BAT.

```
rem *************************** autoexec.bat
rem ****** Start with the universal commands
path c:\dos;c:\wp51;c:\utils
prompt $p$g
lh c:\mouse1\mouse.com


rem ****** Branch based on config variable.
goto %config%


rem ******* Executed only if DOS selected
rem ******* in config.sys.
:dos
doskey
```

```
rem ****** Run the menu.bat batch program.
c:\dos\menu


rem ****** Executed only if Windows selected
rem ****** in config.sys.
:windows
c:\dos\smartdrv.exe
win
goto end


rem ****** Executed only if Network selected
rem ****** in config.sys
:network
ipx
netx
f:
login honcho
c:
prompt [NET]$p$g


:end
```

Notice that, in the above example, the section labeled **:dos** contains the command **c:\dos\menu**. That command shows how you can automatically execute a custom menu, like MENU.BAT described earlier, at startup. If you chose DOS from the configuration options, this AUTOEXEC.BAT file would automatically run the batch program named MENU.BAT on the C:\DOS directory.

Autoexecute Your Custom Menu

Other Commands in AUTOEXEC.BAT

Here's a quick overview of other commands you're likely to find in your own AUTOEXEC.BAT file. Remember, you can get more information on any command by typing **help** followed by a space and the command you want help with.

PATH

This command tells DOS which drives and directories to search for program files (.BAT, .COM, and .EXE) if it can't find a requested program on the current directory.

DOS searches directories as listed (from left-to-right). To maximize system performance, list the most frequently accessed directories first.

Be sure to separate individual directories in a PATH statement by semicolons (;) and do not type any blank spaces. DOS interprets a blank space as the end of the list! So if you modify the PATH command yourself, remember that the only blank space allowed in the command is the one that follows the word PATH, and that a semicolon separates each drive\directory in the list.

PROMPT

This command defines the appearance of the command prompt. For example, the common setting

```
prompt $p$g
```

displays the current drive and directory followed by a greater-than sign (>).

LOADHIGH or LH

If you ran the new DOS 6 utility MemMaker, chances are your AUTOEXEC.BAT file may contain one or more LOADHIGH (or abbreviated LH) commands. LOADHIGH just tells DOS to load a program or device driver into upper memory, rather than conventional memory, as discussed in Step 13.

CALL

Normally when a batch program includes a command that runs another batch program, all batch processing stops after the called batch file finishes. For example, in my sample AUTOEXEC.BAT file, it's not necessary to follow the **c:\dos\menu** command with a **goto end** command, because once MENU.BAT takes over, it won't return to AUTOEXEC.BAT.

Sometimes, you might want to have one batch program run another, then resume with its own commands. In that case, you need to precede the startup command with CALL. For example, this command:

```
call c:\dos\macros.bat
```

in a batch program would execute all the commands in MACROS.BAT. After all those commands have finished, DOS would return to the commands in the current batch program, starting with the first command beneath the CALL command.

Run one batch program from another

Step 20

Problems and Solutions

 15

While it's true that many things can go wrong when you use a computer, most problems can be solved quickly and easily. A cool head will help you resist the urge to throw your computer out the nearest window every time you feel stuck. In this step, we'll look at some common DOS error messages, and ways to deal with them when they arise.

The first thing to do when you're stuck or stymied is to *look to the screen for any error messages, information, or options about how to correct the problem.* If you're in the Shell, you can typically press F1, or click on the Help command button, to get more information.

Look to the screen for information

But many DOS error messages are far from self-explanatory. This step lists the most common error messages, with a brief description of what could cause the error and how to solve the problem.

Abort, Ignore, Retry, Fail? or **Abort, Retry, Fail?** Another message usually appears above this one, telling you what went wrong. Often a disk or device error has occurred. This part of the message is a list of options. Type the first letter of the option you want:

A   Abort and end the program or command.

I   Ignore the problem and continue. Selecting Ignore may result in some lost data. This option is not available for floppy disk errors.

R   Retry the operation. Choose this option to try again after you've fixed the problem (for example, after you've correctly inserted a disk in a floppy drive or removed a write-protect tab from a disk).

F   Fail (end) the current operation and continue with the next one.

Access denied   You've tried to replace or erase a write-protected, read-only, or locked file. If you're working with a floppy, make sure the disk isn't write-protected. Also, use the ATTRIB command at the command prompt, or File ⇒ Change Attributes in the Shell, to deactivate the file's Read Only attribute.

Are you sure (Y/N)?   You've used the wildcard *.* with the DEL or ERASE commands to delete all files in a directory. Type N if you *don't* want to delete all the files. Type Y only if you're sure you want to delete all the files.

Bad command or file name   The command you typed is not available because you've misspelled it, it's never been installed on your computer, or it's not available in the current PATH.

If you're trying to run a program that you know is on the disk, you're probably trying to run it from the wrong directory. Switch to the program's home directory using the CD command, then try again. Or try running the program from the File List in the Shell.

If you're at the command prompt and want to know which directories are in your PATH statement, just type **path** and press ⏎. You can change the PATH command by editing your AUTOEXEC.BAT file.

Common typos   If you're not trying to run a program from the wrong directory, or trying to run a nonexistent program, chances are you've simply mistyped the command. Check your typing carefully, and try again. Common mistakes to look out for include:

- Misspellings (*dirt* instead of *dir*).

- Typing a forward slash (/) where you should have typed a backslash (\), or vice versa.

- Typing a semicolon (;) where you should have typed a colon (:) or vice versa.

- Omitting a space character (**prompt$p$g**) where you need one (**prompt pg**), or putting a space (**path c:\dos; c:\windows**) where one doesn't belong (**path c:\dos;c:\windows**). Review the proper syntax for the command using **help** or **/?**. Keep in mind that any blank spaces shown in the syntax of the command are usually required in the command you type.

Bad Command or Parameters You've used an incorrect syntax on the DEVICE or DEVICEHIGH line of CONFIG.SYS. Correct the problem there and restart your system.

Bad or missing Command Interpreter DOS cannot find the file COMMAND.COM in the root directory, the file is invalid, or it has been moved from the directory it was in when you started DOS. Restart the system with a disk that contains a valid copy of COMMAND.COM, or copy the file from your backup DOS master disk (boot disk) to the disk used to start DOS.

This message can also appear if the SHELL command in CONFIG.SYS refers to a nonexistent COMMAND.COM. Correct the problem in CONFIG.SYS and restart your computer.

Bad or missing *filename* You've specified a device incorrectly in the CONFIG.SYS file. Correct the error and restart your computer.

Beep (incessant) If you hear non-stop beeping, you have probably held down a key too long, or something is leaning on your keyboard. Just wait for the problem to correct itself.

Cannot start COMMAND.COM, exiting DOS has run out of file handles. Restart DOS. If the message persists, increase the FILES= setting in CONFIG.SYS and restart your computer.

Convert lost chains to files (Y/N)? CHKDSK has found a problem with the file allocation table and wants permission to store the recovered information in files with the name FILE*nnnn*.CHK. Type Y (for Yes) to convert the information to files, or N (for No) to free the lost data without storing it. Corrections are made only if you included the /F switch on the CHKDSK command line.

Corrections will not be written to disk The disk contains errors, but CHKDSK cannot correct them because you did not include the

/F switch. Type the CHKDSK command again, this time with the /F switch.

Current drive is no longer valid>   You selected Abort after DOS was unable to read the current drive. Type a valid drive letter and colon (for example, **c:**) and press ⏎ to make that drive the current drive.

Data error reading drive *x*:   DOS could not read the data from the disk, most likely due to a defective disk. Try typing **R** (for Retry) a few times when the *Abort, Retry, Fail?* message appears, or type A (for Abort). It's a good idea to make a new copy of this disk, because you may lose information if it's defective.

***xxxxxxx* device driver cannot be initialized**   *See* **Bad command or parameters** above.

Disk error reading (or writing) drive *x*:   *See* **Data error reading drive *x*** above.

Drive not ready   Most likely, you're trying to switch to a floppy disk or CD ROM drive that has no disk in it. Put in a disk and try again. Or, switch back to the hard disk.

Duplicate file name or file not found   You've tried to rename a file to a file name that exists already, or the file you're trying to rename doesn't exist. The syntax is RENAME *oldname newname*. Use the DIR command or DOS Shell to check names of files on the current directory.

Errors found, F parameter not specified
Corrections will not be written to disk   *See* **Corrections will not be written to disk** above.

File allocation table bad   The disk may be defective. Run CHKDSK /F to check and repair the disk.

File cannot be copied onto itself   You're trying to copy or replace a file and have specified the same file name for the source and the target files (the source and target file names must be different).

File creation error   One of the following is wrong:

- The file you're trying to create exists already as a regular file, a directory name, or a hidden or system file.
- Or the root directory is full or out of file names.
- Or (most likely) there is not enough space on the disk for the file.

You can use the DIR or CHKDSK command to see how much space is available on the disk you're trying to write to. If the problem is simply insufficient disk space, either erase unnecessary files to make more room or use a different floppy.

File not found   You've tried to access a file that isn't on the current directory. Check your spelling, and make sure you're on the correct directory. To locate the file, use the Shell or the command syntax **dir** *filename* /s (where *filename* is the name of the file you're looking for).

File was destroyed by the virus   Anti-Virus discovered a file damaged by a virus and cannot recover it. You'll be asked if you want to delete the file (later, you can restore the file from an uninfected backup).

General failure reading (or writing) drive *x*:   Often occurs if you try to read from or write to a floppy disk that has not been formatted yet. Type **R** (for Retry) or **A** (for Abort) when the *Abort, Retry, Fail?* message appears. If necessary, use FORMAT to format the floppy disk.

Incorrect DOS Version   The command cannot run on the version of DOS you are running at the moment. You may need to restart the computer, install versions of the command that match the DOS version, or make sure DOS is retrieving your command from the correct directory or search path.

If you simply copied DOS 6 files from installed floppy startup disks to your hard disk, you might see this message when you try to run an external DOS command from the hard disk. Unfortunately, copying the DOS 6 files to your hard disk manually isn't enough—you'll also need to install the updated DOS 6 system tracks onto your hard disk. To install the required system tracks, reboot from the DOS 6 floppy startup disk. Then enter the **ver** command to confirm that you've booted the DOS version that the commands on your hard disk need. Next, enter the command **sys a: c:** to copy the system tracks from drive A to drive C. Finally, remove the floppy disk, reboot, and use the VER command again to confirm that you're booting from the updated version of DOS.

The "Incorrect DOS Version" message probably *won't* appear if you followed the DOS 6 installation procedures given in Step 1 of this book. Those procedures set up the system tracks for you automatically.

Insert disk with command.com in drive *x*:   You need to remove the disk that's currently in drive *x* (most likely, drive A), and replace it with the disk you boot DOS from. Then press the space bar to proceed.

Insert Disk *y* in drive *x*:   Typically shown during installation programs, this is simply asking to remove the disk that's currently in drive *x*. Put in the requested disk, then press ↵. If this message persists, first make sure that you did indeed insert the correct disk.

If you're installing from backup floppies, and this message persists, chances are that the backup floppies do not have the same volume labels as the original floppies. You can use the LABEL command to check the original volume labels, and to label the backup floppies. If you use DISKCOPY, rather than COPY, to create backup disks, you won't have this problem because DISKCOPY copies the volume label.

Insufficient disk space   The disk is full and does not contain enough room to perform the operation. You'll either need to free up space on this disk, or retry the operation on another disk that has sufficient space.

Insufficient memory   Your computer does not have enough memory to perform the operation. Remove memory resident programs and try again, or try using MemMaker to configure memory more efficiently. If that doesn't work, you may need to install more memory.

Internal stack overflow
System Halted   The system tried to use more stacks (memory areas) than were available to handle hardware interrupts. Try restarting DOS, then edit CONFIG.SYS and allocate more stack resources. Type **help stacks** for more information.

Invalid directory   You've tried to switch to a nonexistent directory, or used the wrong syntax in a CD command. If the directory is above the current level, precede the directory path with a backslash, as in **cd \wp51** to get to the wp51 directory. Optionally, use the Shell to locate the directory.

Invalid drive specification   You've specified an invalid drive name. Retype the command with the correct drive letter.

Invalid file name   A file name can be no more than eight characters in length, followed by a period and up to three more characters. You can't use blank spaces, nor any of the characters " / [ ] * | ; > + = , ? in a file name. You can use : and \ only as part of the overall path (for example, C:\DOS\MYFILE.PRG).

Invalid media, track 0 bad or unusable   The disk that you're trying to format is faulty, or you're trying to format a low-density disk as a high-density disk. If the problem is the latter, you can use the /f switch with the FORMAT command to format to a lower density. For example, **format a: /f:360** or **format b: /f:720**.

Invalid switch or **invalid parameters:**   You've probably made a typo. Check the syntax using **help** or **/?**. And see **Bad command or file name** above for common typographical errors.

Label not found   Your batch program contains a GOTO command that has no corresponding label. Open the batch program with an editor, type the label correctly (with the leading :), save your changes, and try running the program again.

x **lost cluster(s) found in** *y* **chains** *See* **Convert lost chains to files (Y/N)?** above.

No path You've entered the PATH command to check the current path, but there isn't a defined path. Either no path was defined in AUTOEXEC.BAT, or you bypassed AUTOEXEC.BAT at the start of this session. You also may have cleared the path by typing **path;** (to create your own PATH command, edit AUTOEXEC.BAT).

Non-DOS disk error reading (or writing) drive *x*: DOS cannot recognize the disk format because the disk is missing information or contains another operating system. Try running CHKDSK /F. If this fails, you may need to use FORMAT to reformat the disk (this will destroy files on the disk).

Non-System disk or disk error
Replace and press any key when ready You restarted your computer with a non-system disk in the floppy drive. Remove the floppy disk (or replace it with a DOS startup disk) and press any key to continue.

Not ready error reading (or writing) drive *x*: You've probably left the floppy disk drive door open or inserted the floppy disk upside down, backwards, or sideways. Correct the problem and type **R** (for Retry) when the *Abort, Retry, Fail?* message appears.

Out of environment space You've probably issued a SET command and DOS is out of environment space. Clear variables from the environment by typing the command **SET** *variable=*. Alternatively, you can increase the environment space available by using the /e:*nnnnn* switch on the COMMAND or SHELL= line of CONFIG.SYS, then restart your computer.

Packed file corrupt All or a portion of a program has been loaded in the first 64K of conventional memory and cannot run successfully. Precede the command with **loadfix** and a space. For example, use **loadfix myprog** to run a program named MYPROG.

Parameters not compatible You've specified command switches that cannot be used together. Type **help** *command* to determine which switches are valid for the command.

Please insert disk *x* in drive *x*... *See* **Insert Disk *y* in drive *x*** above.

Program is trying to modify system memory The Vsafe utility has detected that a program is trying to modify the system memory without using the standard DOS calls for memory-resident (TSR) programs. This could mean that a virus is trying to infect your system, although some network drivers can elicit this message from Vsafe when they load. Run Anti-Virus if you suspect a virus invasion.

Program is trying to stay resident in memory You've selected the Resident option, and Vsafe has detected that another program is trying to load into memory. This could signal a possible virus infection. If you're suspicious, run Anti-Virus.

Program is trying to write to disk You've selected the General Write Protect option in Vsafe and a program is trying to write to disk. This could signal a possible virus infection. If you're suspicious, run Anti-Virus.

Program too big to fit in memory *See* **Insufficient memory** above.

Read fault error writing drive *x*: *See* **Unrecoverable read** (or write) error on drive *x*:, below.

Sector not found error reading (or **writing**) **drive *x*:** The disk probably has a bad spot that prevents DOS from finding the requested information. Copy all files from the disk onto a good disk, then use FORMAT to reformat the bad disk (or better yet, throw the bad disk away). Some data may be lost if the bad sector contained information.

Sharing violation reading drive *x*: A program tried to access a file that another program is using. Type **A** (for Abort) or wait a while and type **R** (for Retry).

Terminate batch job (Y/N)? You've pressed Ctrl+C or Ctrl+Break to interrupt a batch program. To stop the program, type **Y** (for Yes); to continue the program where it left off, type **N** (for No).

This program requires Microsoft Windows   You're trying to run a Windows program from DOS. Precede the command with **win** and a blank space. For example, enter **win a:setup** rather than just **a:setup**. Or run the program from the Windows File Manager or choose File ⟹ Run in the Windows Program Manager.

Too many parameters   You've probably included a space in a file or path name, or a semicolon after a drive letter. Retype the command correctly. See **Bad command or file name** for common typographical errors.

Too many files open   The FILES= setting in CONFIG.SYS is too low. Edit CONFIG.SYS, increase the maximum number of open files, then reboot and try again.

Unable to create directory   You tried to create a directory that already exists, or the disk is full.

Unrecognized command in CONFIG.SYS   There's an invalid command in CONFIG.SYS. Correct the error and restart your system.

Unrecoverable read (or write) **error on drive** *x:*   DOS cannot read from or write to the disk because the floppy disk is inserted upside down, backwards, or sideways. Correct the problem and type **R** (for Retry).

WARNING: ALL DATA ON NON-REMOVABLE DISK DRIVE *x:* **WILL BE LOST!**
Proceed with Format (Y/N)?   You are trying to format a hard disk. Type **N** (for No) unless you are absolutely sure that you want to permanently delete *everything* on the hard disk.

Verify Error   Anti-Virus has discovered a change in an executable file, which may or may not be caused by a virus. You can repair the attribute, time, or date; delete the file if you suspect a virus caused the change; update Anti-Virus's statistics to suppress future messages about this file if the change was legitimate; or continue to the next file.

Virus Found   Anti-Virus has found a virus. Your best bet is to eradicate the virus with the Clean button.

Write fault error writing drive *x*:   *See* **Unrecoverable read (or write) error on drive *x*:** above.

Write protect error writing drive *x*:   You've tried to write to a floppy disk that is write-protected. Remove the write-protect tab on a 5.25" disk, or close the write-protect slide on a 3.5" disk. Then press **R** (for Retry) in response to the *Abort, Retry, Fail?* message.

Wrong disk in drive...   *See* **Insert Disk *y* in drive *x*** above.

Index

Note: **Boldface** page numbers in this index show where you'll find the steps for an important DOS operation or the primary discussion of a major topic. *Italic* page numbers identify illustrations.